Make Your Words Count

a

SHORT painless GUIDE™

to Business Writing for Accountants

by

Helen Wilkie

Make Your Words Count: a Short Painless Guide to Business Writing for Accountants

This book is available at a special discount for bulk purchase by your group, company, organization or professional association for sales or event promotions, premiums, fundraising or professional development workshops given by Helen Wilkie.

For details please call 416-966-5023
or email hwilkie@mhwcom.com

Short Painless Guides are published by

MHW Communications of Toronto, Canada

MHW
COMMUNICATIONS

Praise for *Make Your Words Count* from accounting professionals:

"This book is a great tool that met my expectations. It's an easy read and a great resource for any accountant, especially those who are fortunate enough to take Helen's business writing course."

Marc Rouleau, CA, CFE
Vice-President
WelchGroup Consulting, a subsidiary of Welch LLP

"Your approach is great! You do a great job in illustrating poor writing and vastly improved rewrites."

Adam Rubinoff, BMath, CA
Partner, Taxation Group
Soberman LLP

"Helen is a master communicator, and her book is a must read for every accounting professional. I am amazed how Helen, although not a professional accountant herself, really understands our mindset. A good illustration of this for me was the *Simplifying the Complex* section. Thank you Helen."

Bruce Singer, CA
CEO
PTC Accounting and Finance Inc.

"Accountants need to communicate complex material, so it is vitally important that their writing be simple and clear. This *Short Painless Guide* is full of information that will help."

Delmarie Scherloski
Vice-President
Certified General Accountants of Ontario

"Like it or not, people make judgements about you based on your writing. I've seen so many intelligent financial people flounder because they cannot communicate effectively in writing. Finally, here's a book targeted directly at narrowing the gap between what accountants know and how they communicate it."

Merge Gupta-Sunderji, MBA, CGA, CSP

Acknowledgements

I am indebted to all those who reviewed the manuscript and suggested improvements.

I owe a special word of thanks to Jim McConnery, CA, TEP, Tax Partner at Welch LLP of Ottawa, Canada. Jim patiently worked with me to ensure that my "Simplifying the Complex" examples were technically correct from a tax standpoint.

Finally, as always, thanks to Lois Ferguson and Susan Birkenshaw, my "Butt Kickers", who pushed me to start the book and eventually to finish it.

Table of Contents

About this Book 6

How the Book is Arranged 8

Why Accountants Must Write Well 10

What Does Good Business Writing Look Like? 13

Words: the Building Blocks of the Message 14

The Sentence: Engine of the Message 23

Paragraphs: Both Science and Art 36

Jargon: How to Baffle Clients 48

Grammar: Three Principles You Just Have to Know 56

Punctuation without Tears 64

Email: the Particular Writing Challenges 71

Report Writing the DESIGN IT™ Way 76

Editing for Impact 103

Simplifying the Complex 112

In Closing 127

About the Author 129

About This Book

The world doesn't need another heavy tome about business writing, and as an accountant you certainly don't want to spend endless hours reading about writing skills. At the same time, those writing skills have a direct effect on your professional success. That's why I wrote this Short Painless Guide, which you can read quickly and then use as a reference when you need it.

One thing you'll probably notice right away is that some of the writing is ungrammatical.

What? How can a writer on writing commit such a crime? Well the reason is that I want you to "hear" my voice as you read the book, because that's the shortest route to the brain, and often we break the rules of grammar when we speak. People who take my writing courses and programs tell me they appreciate the way I keep the tone light, while at the same time taking the subject seriously, so I've tried to follow the same course with the book.

I wouldn't take this approach, however, in writing a business letter or report, as those call for a higher level of formality.

With grammar, as with other areas of life, you need to know the rules so that you can decide when it's OK to break them. (That's my story and I'm sticking to it, so please don't write in!)

How the Book Is Arranged

Before I get into the meat and potatoes of the book, I've given you my thoughts on why you should care about good writing and what that actually looks like. I've kept it brief, because I think it's important and I want you to read it. (This is a sentiment you might keep in mind in your own writing!)

We begin with the building blocks of the written message: words, sentences and paragraphs, because you need to have a grasp of these principles in order to write well. After all, if you don't know how to put the bricks together, you won't have a very good wall.

Want to know how to baffle your clients? Read the section on jargon.

This is not a comprehensive grammar course. There are, however, a few grammar principles you just need to know, and you'll find them on page 56.

There are several types of message you, as an accountant, normally write. If I expounded on them all in detail, though, this would no longer be a Short Painless Guide and you'd probably be comatose by the time I finished. Fortunately, you can use the general writing principles in most of these situations. For the purposes of the book, I'll zero in on just two subjects: email and report writing.

Next there are some thoughts on the art of self-editing, with some before and after examples that show the impact of good editing even on good writing.

One group of people accountants must often address their messages to is—non-accountants! These messages are often complex, and it's important that they be couched in terms the reader can reasonably be expected to understand—see my remarks below about client service. Hence the final section on simplifying the complex.

I've made it short and painless, so you've no excuse for putting the book on a shelf to gather dust. Don't be misled by its brevity and tone though, because there's gold in them there pages! (It's a joke—don't write in.) I hope you'll read it all the way through, make some notes and plan to incorporate the ideas into your everyday on-the-job writing. Then I suggest you return to it from time to time to revisit specific areas of concern to you.

If you were to show me your copy of the book a few months or years from now, I'd like to see it dog-eared from much use.

Happy Writing!
Helen Wilkie
Toronto, Canada

Why Accountants Must Write Well

This is my second attempt at this section. When I gave the first one to a friend for her opinion, she told me it was boring! Never let it be said that I wrote a boring book, and in fact it was this comment that led me to the whole Short Painless Guide idea. So if you don't like the format and style, blame my friend Susan.

But no matter how you say it, there are three very real reasons why accountants must write well. Here they are:

- Client service
- Sales and marketing
- Professional reputation

Client service

Whether you're an auditor or a tax specialist, a risk management consultant or a corporate finance guru, you spend a great deal of your time working on client projects and communicating with clients.

At some point during the process, clients expect some advice: what to do next, how to correct a problem, how to deal with the tax authorities. And they expect to be able to understand that advice.

In my work with accounting firms, I've seen many client letters filled with large chunks of text quoted directly from the Income Tax Act, with very little explanation of what it actually means to the client. (I don't work with the people who actually draft this legislation, as they are clearly beyond my help.) I don't need my accountant to quote chapter and verse; I need him to guide me through the process by advising me in plain English.

If your client reads your report and doesn't understand the advice you are providing, you have not served your client.

Sales and Marketing

We live in a world filled with selling and marketing messages, directed both at consumers and at business people. But if we're going to succeed in business, we must market all the time, and accounting firms are not immune to this need. Like other professionals, though, your challenge is to communicate the benefits you have to offer clients in such a way that they not only understand them, but see you as a firm they actually want to work with.

If several accounting firms are courting the same potential client, either through the written word or oral presentations, or both, the one that communicates its message in the most clear and compelling way will more often than not win the business.

Professional Reputation

Every time you send a written message to anyone outside your firm, you are representing your firm. In fact, you *are* your firm to that person at that time. The quality of your writing, therefore, has an impact on how your firm is perceived by those on the outside.

I shudder to think of the impression conveyed every day by ineffective (not to mention ungrammatical) email messages, rambling reports and other disasters. I'm not saying you are one of the guilty ones, but I've seen these examples, so I know they are out there.

On the other hand, good writing enhances a firm's reputation by conveying an impression of professionalism, competence and confidence.

What Does Good Business Writing Look Like?

I like to think of good writing as transparent, much like good acting. If you are watching a movie or a play and you turn to your friend and say, "Isn't he a great actor?", then in my mind it's not really good acting. If the acting is good, you shouldn't even notice the actor, but rather see the character he or she is playing.

Similarly, good writing helps the reader focus on the message without actually noticing the words. Like acting, though, that doesn't happen automatically. It's the effort that goes into planning the message and then expressing it in appropriate terms that produces the desired result. The purpose of this Short Painless Guide is to help you learn how to accomplish this result as simply as possible.

That said, let's get to work.

Words: the Building Blocks of the Message

Words are the basic building blocks of the written message. We start using words when we're little children, so by the time we come to write business messages we're pretty comfortable with a huge number of them. We don't have to think about most of these words consciously because our brains send them directly out of our mouths in a way that makes sense.

But this doesn't quite cover it when it comes to business writing. Here, we need to actually think about the words we're using. Here are three principles to follow in choosing your words:

1. Use simple words
2. Cut out the fluff
3. Use the right word in the right place

1. Please don't misunderstand me. I don't mean you should write in kindergarten level words of one syllable—at least

not all the time. Somebody in one of my workshops told me he didn't want to *dumb down* his message because he was writing to intelligent people. First of all, I find the expression *dumb down* offensive, because it suggests a certain arrogance towards those we consider less smart than ourselves. That's not what this is about at all.

When you write a series of complicated, obscure "ten dollar words" in a single sentence, people's eyes glaze over. They might understand each word individually, but when you pile them up one after another like that, they just get in the way of the overall message. Aim for a mix of levels of complexity in words, and when in doubt err on the side of simplicity.

2. Have you ever heard the old expression, *You can't see the wood for the trees*? You're looking at so many trees that you don't see the actual wood they're made of. That's what happens when you write lots of words, many of which are unnecessary. When your sentences are full of *in order to, as a consequence, as such* etc., you can't see the message for the words. Get rid of useless words that add nothing to the meaning.

3. Nothing will destroy your credibility faster than using a word incorrectly. It might be a perfectly good word, but it doesn't mean what you think it does, so your sentence doesn't make sense. Bottom line: never use a word unless you are 100% sure you know its meaning and are using it correctly in context.

Let's look at some examples of these three principles of word use.

Simple Words Can Say It Best

As I mentioned a moment ago, no matter how well educated we are, or how many words we know and understand, when confronted with a sentence completely made up of what I call "ten dollar words", our eyes tend to glaze over.

If you doubt that, take a look at this sentence:

> *In performing the tax accounting services for which you have engaged us, we depend upon the veracity and comprehensive nature of all data and information furnished to us, and do not undertake to verify, clarify or otherwise investigate such underlying data or its support materials.*

Huh?

As an experiment to prove this point, a friend once inserted a series of six high-flown words into a sentence in an internal memo to a colleague. In a discussion afterwards, it was clear that the recipient didn't even notice that the sentence made no sense at all. Why? Because his eye (and his brain) simply skimmed over the words instead of trying to interpret them!

Some professionals believe that if they use simple words, people will think they are unsophisticated or even uneducated. If that's what you think, you're wrong. If you write in simple words, people won't even notice the words because they'll be too busy getting the message. And isn't that the whole point of the exercise?

Here are just a few potentially too complicated words and

expressions, with possible simple alternatives. You needn't eliminate the words on the left from your writing, but consider using the simpler version on the right often enough to be sure your meaning comes through loud and clear.

Instead of this	***Try this***
utilize	use
forward	send
transpire	occur, happen
aggregate	total
furnish	give, send, provide
initiate	begin, start
optimum	best
the undersigned	I, me
designate	appoint, choose

Too Many Words

Of all the writing problems I find in my live workshops for accountants (and pretty much everyone else for that matter), this one is the most common: too many words!

Somehow in our attempt to be businesslike, or maybe it's to make sure we cover all the bases, we load our sentences up with wordy phrases that don't add anything to the meaning. I have a theory about this. I believe it comes from university days, when we were told to write a paper with X words. They said 2500 words, but they didn't specify they had to be 2500 working words that served a purpose. So we all became experts at padding! Sound familiar?

Fast forward now to the real world, the world of business. Nobody is counting your words now. Your colleagues, your senior partner, your clients—nobody cares that you wrote a specific number of words. What they care about is receiving and understanding the message your words convey.

But old habits die hard, and many accountants still write as if they have to meet a word count, resulting in phrases like the ones in the left column below. Cut away the dead wood, the words that add nothing, and we get the clearer meaning of those on the right.

Instead of this	***Try this***
as you may or may not know	as you may know, as you may not know
at this point in time	now, at present
for the simple reason that	because
in the neighbourhood of	about, approximately
ten feet in length	ten feet, ten feet long
in the event that	if
it is our recommendation	we recommend
I would like to suggest	I suggest
under separate cover	separately
made an analysis of	analyzed

So just in this small sampling, we've gone from 45 to about 20 words, cutting out more than 50% of the original word count. Now that may not seem like much, but consider it in the context of, say, an audit report. How many pages is your average audit report? How many could it be if you cut out words at this rate?

And cutting out extra words doesn't just cut down the length of the written message—it actually makes it clearer.

I once read a story about the famous sculptor Michelangelo. Someone apparently asked him how he managed to create those beautiful angels out of a lump of cold, hard marble. Michelangelo is reputed to have replied, "I just chip away anything that's not angel, and the angel emerges."

So chip away the words that are not necessary, and your message will emerge.

Stop Saying the Same Things Twice

In the last section I dealt with the problem of too many words, or what I call fluff. There's another form of fluff that's very common in business writing: redundancy. What do I mean by that? I mean those phrases we write without thinking about them, and without stopping to realize they actually say the same thing twice. Here are just a few examples:

1. 10 a.m. in the morning
2. new breakthrough
3. necessary requisite
4. absolutely perfect
5. very unique
6. the future ahead
7. past history
8. foreign import

Really *think* about what I've just written in these words.

1. Come on, I don't need to explain the first one, do I? 10 a.m. or 10 o'clock in the morning—choose one.

2. Have you ever heard of an old breakthrough? *Breakthrough* is a great word that suggests something new and exciting—let it speak for itself.
3. If it's necessary, it's a requisite—and vice versa.
4. The word *perfect* is an absolute: a thing is either perfect or it's not.
5. *Unique* is a word we've stolen from the French language and then we've spoiled it. Unique doesn't mean unusual: it means one of a kind. Something is either unique or it's very unusual.
6. The future ahead? Where else would it be?
7. History, by definition, is past.
8. What's an import? Something that comes from foreign parts. Again, let the word speak for itself.

Why do we do this? Again, I have a theory. I believe much of what we write in the course of our jobs comes through our fingers onto the keyboard, through the computer onto the printer and finally onto the paper—completely bypassing the brain! We write these words every day and we never think about them.

So if there's one big change you can make right now that will improve the clarity of your writing, it's this: think about what you are writing. Read what you've just written and consider whether it makes sense, whether it's full of redundant words that just take up space for no reason. And when you find them, cut them out.

Use the Right Word in the Right Place

English is a rich language—we have more words than we

know what to do with. Some pairs of words look similar, as if they would mean the same thing, but they don't. Sometimes there's just a shade of difference in meaning, and sometimes they are completely different.

Here are some that are habitually used incorrectly, with the correct usage beneath.

We must consider the affect of the capital cost allowance.
We must consider the effect of the capital cost allowance.
The capital cost allowance affected our profits for the year.

As a visitor, I am disinterested in the election results.
As a visitor, I am uninterested in the election results.
As an election official, I must be a disinterested party.

The accountant made an error in the estimate, but the amount was negligent.
The accountant made an error in the estimate, but the amount was negligible.
The accountant was negligent in making an error in the estimate.

The client inferred that he would take his business elsewhere.
The client implied that he would take his business elsewhere.
From his voicemail message, I inferred that the client would take his business elsewhere.

The team was in jeopardy of losing the game.
The team was in danger of losing the game.
The game was in jeopardy.

Oh, you thought I was going to explain each one? No no no, you can check the meanings in your dictionary. I'm not doing all the work for you. (You're the student here—don't write in.)

If you use the wrong word in context, it can do terrible things to your credibility, which in turn can affect your career or your business. Use a dictionary, either online or paper version, if you're in any doubt about the meaning of a word. If doubt remains, find a different word.

Master the use of words, and the impact of your writing will automatically increase.

The Sentence: Engine of the Message

The sentence is the engine of the message, and when you get it right you're halfway there. But what does it mean to "get it right"? What is a "right" sentence?

Well it goes without saying (although I'll say it anyway) that it should be grammatically correct, but that's just the beginning. If words are the building blocks of the message, sentences are the walls, and walls don't just have to look good: they have to hold up the building. An effective sentence clearly conveys its own part of the overall message, contributing in turn to a solid, logical written piece.

I'm not going to talk about grammar here, because there's a separate section for that later. ("Oh no," I hear you say! But trust me, you'll thank me later.)

Let me talk first about a basic power sentence. Isn't that a great term? I wish I had thought of it, but I didn't. (If I knew who did coin the phrase I'd be happy to give them credit, but I don't—all I know is it's a great term.) I like it because it seems to describe what we should be striving for in business writing: power.

A power sentence has certain characteristics:

- It uses the active voice
- It contains specific words
- It uses action verbs
- Its core is together

In the next four sections I'll look at each of these in detail.

Power Sentences: Active Voice

If you use a grammar checker on your computer, you may have seen a dialog box that said, "Is this a passive construction and do you want to change it?" Many people have confessed to me that they never touch this because they don't know what it means. Well, if that's you, you're about to find out.

The voice of a sentence has nothing to do with past, present or future. That's tense. The voice is created through the placement of the three main parts of the sentence: the subject, the verb and the object. (Yes, I know I said no grammar, but this won't take a moment and I need to talk about it so that this section will make sense.)

The subject is the person or thing taking the action, the verb is the action and the object is the person or thing being acted upon.

In the active voice, they appear in that order: subject, verb, object. Here's an example:

The auditor (subject) completed (verb) the report (object).

If English is your native tongue, this is how you learned to speak. Writing in the active voice creates the natural, forward motion of the language.

It is possible, though, to reverse this order and write object, verb, subject—like this:

The report was written by the auditor.

This order is called the passive voice. It's grammatically correct and perfectly acceptable—but it's back to front. It's not natural, and it slows down the pace of the sentence, often to the point of tedium when overused. And my goodness, it's overused! It's generally thought that for reasonable levels of comprehension and interest, we should aim for a ratio of active to passive voice of about 75/25. Unfortunately, most business writing is almost the reverse.

And the result? Well I mentioned tedium and that's certainly one result. Try this experiment and you'll see what I mean. Pull out a written piece that you found particularly boring, and I can almost guarantee it's predominantly in passive voice.

Why do we do this? Well, there are two reasons.

First, for some strange reason we think it sounds more businesslike. This is why people tend to think business writing is boring, when it doesn't have to be.

The other reason is a little sneaky. There's another form of the passive voice in which the subject is omitted altogether, as in:

Your application will be processed immediately.

Oh really? And who'll be doing that? We don't say. This form is called (and I'm not making this up) the Divine Passive!

I think you can see the attraction of this form. You can make statements without taking responsibility or ownership for them. I'm not saying I will process the application, or indeed that any specific person will. I'm just saying it will be done. (Divine, remember?)

The problem is that if you do this too much, your reader will get a subliminal message that all is not as it seems and you can inadvertently create a feeling of distrust.

So take a look at something you've written recently and consider the ratio of active to passive voice. Too much passive? Try turning as many passive voice sentences as possible into active voice, and you'll see a huge difference in the impact of your writing.

Power Sentences: Specific Words

English is a rich language. Without necessarily using the ten dollar words I talked about in another section, we can always find a word or phrase that says exactly what we want to say. So why do we so often use vague words that leave room for misunderstanding or confusion? Maybe we don't realize we're being vague, or maybe we're just lazy.

I call these non-specific descriptors *umbrella* words or phrases, and using them forces your reader to guess the exact meaning. That way lies disaster. Here are some examples.

Document—Was there ever such a generic word? In days of old, before computers, a document was an actual piece of paper with a message on it. But now everything created on a computer is a document, whether or not it finds its way into print.

Material—People are always asking one another to send along material. What is that? Many years ago I used to sew my own clothes out of material. (Are you sending me bolts of cloth?) I saw a store the other day selling artists' materials.

Deal with, handle—umbrella words are not just nouns. They can also be verbs or verb phrases. If you tell me you'll handle the situation, what does that mean? How are you going to deal with the problem? And what are the *situation* and the *problem* anyway? Two more umbrella words!

Power sentences use words that name things and ideas specifically. This avoids confusion—and the tedium that comes from repetition of vague words.

Power Sentences: Action Verbs

When I talk about action verbs, sometimes people tell me they thought all verbs were action words, but that's not the case. A verb can denote an action, such as walk, teach, exercise. But a verb can also describe a state of mind or existence. Such words are called linking verbs, and they are usually a form of the verb *to be*.

Here's an example of a sentence based on a linking verb:

I am a lover of classical music.

The verb is *am*, which doesn't describe an action but a condition or state of mind. The reason it's called a linking verb is that it can't stand on its own—it needs to link to something else in order to have meaning. In this case, it links to *a lover of classical music.*

We can make this sentence more powerful by changing it to an action verb orientation. To do this, we ask a question: if I am a lover of classical music, what do I do? The answer is:

I love classical music.

Love is an action verb.

Some linking verbs are necessary, but their overuse slows down the writing and robs it of impact. Try turning the following sentences around and giving them an action orientation by changing the verb:

Our managing partner is good at solving complex accounting problems. (Our managing partner *solves* complex accounting problems *well.*)

Our firm's services are useful to clients who want to legally minimize their taxes. (Our firm's services *help* clients legally minimize their taxes.)

Can you see how much more impact the resulting sentences have? If you want your writing to have an impact on your reader's mind, write power sentences that use action verbs.

Power Sentences: Core Together

Remember the Grammar 101 lesson from the section on the active voice? I talked about the subject, the verb and the object. When you consider these three components together, they are called the core of the sentence. In a power sentence, the core is together. When the core breaks up and scatters throughout the sentence, the result can be horrible.

Consider this sentence:

We have reviewed the profit and loss statement for last year.

It's a simple sentence with a basic subject (we), verb (have reviewed), object (the profit and loss statement) construction, and it's a perfectly good, grammatically correct sentence. But let's say we want to add some more detail. Here's a sentence from someone's writing sample at one of my workshops:

> *We, in the course of our engagement, have reviewed, as requested in a letter written by the previous owner of the restaurant in order to determine his liability for tax arrears, the profit and loss statement for the last year.*

What a rambling, confused, ugly sentence! Can you see what's happened? Look for the core, and you'll find it scattered throughout the sentence, separated by many other words and ideas.

It's perfectly acceptable to put extra details in a sentence, but you must keep the core together in the interests of clarity, not to mention the elegance of your sentence. Here's a much better version:

> *As requested in a letter written by the previous owner of the restaurant to determine his liability for tax arrears, in the course of our engagement we have reviewed the profit and loss statement for last year.*

Notice we still have all the detail, but we've brought the core of the sentence back together, so the reader doesn't have to search for the meaning. It's right there in the core of the sentence. (It's still not a great sentence, but at least we've made the meaning clearer by moving the core together.)

If you find yourself in the position of reader trying to find your way through a long, rambling sentence like this one, look for the core. When you isolate the core, you'll understand the meaning of the sentence. (Don't make your readers do this though—it's the writer's job.)

Beyond the power sentence

As I've said before, the sentence is the engine of the message, and a grammatically correct power sentence is a good beginning. But there's more to the sentence than that.

If you want to make a point, emphasize one aspect over another or leave your reader with a specific idea uppermost in his or her mind, you can accomplish all that through the structure of your sentences.

Sentences are made up of clauses, each of which must contain a verb. The way we manipulate emphasis in a sentence is by using certain words to create a relationship of subordination among the various clauses.

Let's take a look at how we do this.

Emphasis through Clause Relationship

When one idea is less important than another, we call it a subordinate clause, and we define that by introducing it with a subordinating conjunction. This is usually a single word but can also be a short phrase. Some examples of these are:

although, after, as if, as soon as, because, even if, if, otherwise, since, even though, unless, whenever, despite, as a result.

The following sentences illustrate how we create the relative emphasis through these conjunctions:

> ***Although*** *the company had purchased hockey tickets as a promotional tool, the CRA disallowed the expense.*

What's important? The expense was disallowed.

> ***As soon as*** *we receive the information we requested, we will complete the last phase of your audit.*

The main idea? We will finish the audit.

> ***Due to*** *an error on the part of our accountant, we overpaid our taxes by $2,000.*

The bottom line? We paid too much tax.

We can change the emphasis simply by attaching the subordinating conjunction to the other clause:

> ***Although*** *the CRA disallowed the expense, the company had purchased hockey tickets as a promotional tool.*

What we want to emphasize is the reason the company bought the tickets.

This type of structure can cause problems. If you inadvertently subordinate the wrong clause, your reader's mind can go off in a different direction from what you want. In the editing part of the process, you might feel a certain sentence is not making your point strongly enough. If that's the case, try changing the subordinating relationship and see what happens to the meaning.

Rank the Importance of the Ideas

If there's more than one idea in a sentence, you need to decide which one is most important and structure the sentence to make it stand out. We show the relative importance through the words we use to join them, as well as the order in which we express them. Let's look first at the joining words and phrases. Joining words are called conjunctions (a note for the grammatically inclined).

If the ideas in the sentence are of equal importance or strength, join them using *and, or, but, nor.*

> *I am going to a conference, and I hope to learn something useful.*

We can meet on Thursday or wait until next week.

Mary wants to specialize in tax, but at present she is working on audits.

These sentences are all correct, and if the ideas carry equal weight these are the appropriate structures. The problem is, though, that if we write like this all the time, there's no emphasis, no vigour, no life in the message. It's all right to write the occasional sentence this way, but you must inject some variety if you want your message to have impact.

(By the way, did you notice a difference in the punctuation of the sentences? There is a difference, but I'm not going to go into it now—all will be clear when you read Punctuation Without Tears on page 64. Meanwhile, back to our sentences.)

Change the Order of the Clauses

The order of the clauses, or ideas, also affects the way the reader understands what is important. For example, try to finish your sentence with the thought you want to stick in the reader's mind. Let's consider our previous examples again:

Although the company had purchased hockey tickets as a promotional tool, the CRA disallowed the expense.

What's important? The expense was disallowed.

Depending on the purpose of the message, we might in fact want to emphasize the fact that we are implementing a marketing plan. In that case, we would reverse the order of the ideas:

> *Although the CRA disallowed the expense, the company had purchased hockey tickets as a promotional tool.*

See the difference?

We've not only attached the subordinating conjunction to the other clause, but we've strengthened the emphasis by putting the promotional idea at the end of the sentence.

> *As soon as we receive the information we requested, we will complete the last phase of your audit.*

The main idea? We will finish the audit.

But maybe we want to urge the reader to send us the information so that we can get on with the work. In that case, reverse the order:

> *We will complete the last phase of your audit as soon as you send us the information we requested.*

Here we haven't moved the subordinating conjunction, but by reversing the order of the clauses, we have subtly but clearly suggested that the next move is up to them.

> *Due to an error by our accountant, we overpaid our taxes by $2,000.*

The bottom line? We paid too much tax.

But what if the writer wants to emphasize to his or her boss that this was somebody else's fault? Reverse the order:

> *We overpaid our taxes by $2,000 due to an error by our accountant.*

It's pretty clear here that the writer is blaming the accountant and wants to make that more important than the overpayment.

So we can change the emphasis by moving the subordinating conjunction, reversing the order of the clauses or, usually even more compelling, a combination of the two. Please be sure you understand this, because many a reader has been sent off at a tangent because a sentence emphasized the wrong thing.

Effective sentences drive the meaning of your message.

Paragraphs: Both Science and Art

Paragraphing is part science, part art. There's no set number of sentences in a paragraph, and in fact there can be just one sentence by itself. You don't want to have too many sentences, simply because the paragraph would be too long, and that would make it a barrier to communication.

More important than the number of sentences is the way the sentences are crafted together into a paragraph. Just as we have power sentences, we also have power paragraphs. Whatever the topic, and regardless of length, a power paragraph has the following characteristics:

- Focus
- Unity
- Coherence

Focus

Think of a paragraph as a unit of thought. *One* thought. *One* idea. *One* focus. You might use more than one paragraph to discuss a single idea, but there should never be more than one idea in a paragraph.

The component of a paragraph that creates focus is called by several names:

- The key sentence
- The core sentence
- The topic sentence

These all mean the same thing, and for purposes of this discussion I will use the one I like, the topic sentence.

The topic sentence is usually the first one in the paragraph, although not always. If you are using more than one paragraph to cover your topic, you won't repeat the topic sentence after the first one.

When you go to the theatre, the curtains open and the scenery immediately tells you where the action will take place and gives you some idea of mood. Similarly, the topic sentence sets the scene for the reader of the paragraph.

A good topic sentence should be general but also limiting. What does that mean? Well it needs to be general enough to encompass all the aspects of the information. But if it's too general, it might confuse the reader by offering too much information.

For example, consider this potential topic sentence:

> *Accounting is a wise choice of profession for a young person.*

What would this paragraph talk about? Hard to say, isn't it? I guess it would depend on why the writer held this opinion, but from the reader's standpoint it's not helpful. It doesn't focus the mind. A much better topic sentence would be:

> *Accounting is a wise choice of profession for a young person who takes pride in his or her work and enjoys working on a team of like-minded professionals.*

See the difference? Clearly I'm not going to read about dealing with the tax authorities, making a high salary or having opportunities to live in different parts of the country. No, the topic sentence tells me the paragraph will focus on the importance of pride of workmanship.

Next, having established the topic of the paragraph, we need to keep it focused on that topic.

Unity

We use a topic sentence to focus the paragraph; we keep it focused by creating a sense of unity. This means everything in the paragraph is tied to the specific focus established by the topic sentence.

Any topic you may be discussing is likely to have many aspects, all of which you want to cover in your written message. But it's important to keep these aspects separate to avoid confusion. Remember the rule: one paragraph, one topic.

Let's take the topic sentence I created earlier:

Accounting is a wise choice of profession for a young person who takes pride in his or her work and enjoys working on a team of like-minded professionals.

Here are a number of sentences on the subject of accounting as a career choice:

1. Accountants are highly regarded in the community.
2. Accountants help small business people be successful.
3. Large corporations depend on accountants to keep them compliant with the law.
4. Accounting provides opportunities to produce detailed reports.
5. Being part of the accounting profession will allow you to travel the country and meet your colleagues in the course of your work.
6. Working with clients on their tax issues will help you to handle your own taxes effectively.
7. Accountants have a strong sense of self-worth because of the work they do.
8. As a public accountant, you will work with others who hold the same principles as you do.
9. A career in accounting will allow you to work with a wide variety of people and organizations, including the tax authorities.

They all deal with accounting as a career, but how many belong in a paragraph with this topic sentence? There is usually room for some difference of opinion on this question, but I suggest the following:

1. Possibly
2. Probably not
3. No
4. No
5. No
6. No
7. Yes
8. Yes
9. No

Inserting any of the "no" sentences will destroy the unity of the paragraph.

In discussions about writing, people often talk about a nebulous idea called *flow*. They'll say their writing doesn't flow, or they can't get it to flow, or there's something wrong with the flow. In my experience, problems with flow come down to lack of unity because a sentence is in the wrong paragraph, or in the right paragraph but the wrong order.

When you come to edit your work, make sure your paragraphs are unified behind the focus of the topic sentence.

Coherence

Coherence in a paragraph means the sentences are arranged in logical order and have logical connection from one sentence to the next. The emphasis on logic is intentional, because you, the writer, must help your reader understand the message your are trying to convey and if there is no sense of logic, you won't be able to do this.

Logical Order

The order you choose will depend to a large extent on the purpose of the piece you are writing. Two possible choices are chronological and importance.

Although it does tend to be the least interesting choice, sometimes chronological order is the most useful and logical one. At a certain point in an engagement, for example, you may be writing a report that offers your client a solution to a business problem. It's quite usual to begin by recapping the background or your understanding of the problem. If this is a story of certain occurrences in the past, putting them in chronological order is probably the way to clearly answer the question: what happened?

When using order of importance, you need to decide whether to start with the least important and move through to the most, or vice versa. Again, it depends on your purpose for writing, but having a clear, obvious order is one way to keep your paragraph in flow.

Logical Connection

The words and phrases we use to connect sentences are called transitional markers. I like to think of these as signposts that define the direction your argument or discussion is taking so that the reader can follow the same direction. The chart below gives just a few possible examples of transitional markers and the direction or arrangement they create.

Arrangement	Possible Transitional Markers
Chronological	first, last, then, next, after, in the meantime, finally, eventually, at the present time, after a while
Importance	more importantly, more to the point, to some extent, to a lesser degree
Similarity	in addition, similarly, likewise, in the same way, also
Difference	on the other hand, on the contrary, but, however, nevertheless, still, yet
Conclusion	therefore, hence, for this reason, so, as a result, thus

Transition from one sentence to another is vital to meaning and understanding. Consider the following:

> Taxation of compensation depends to *some extent/in large part/entirely* on whether compensation is for past or future service. In *general/specifically/for example,* when compensation is for future services, the taxpayer will not pay tax on these sums until the service is rendered. *On the other hand/conversely/at the same time/therefore*, if the compensation is for past service, the taxpayer must pay taxes immediately on this amount regardless of when the compensation was received.

The words in italics represent multiple choices for transitional markers, and if you try the sentence with each one in turn you'll see that the meaning is quite different in each case. If you use the wrong transition, you can not only destroy the flow but also confuse or mislead your reader.

Beyond the Power Paragraph

As we've seen, a power paragraph must have the characteristics of focus, unity and coherence. But the role of the paragraph in an effective written message goes beyond this.

Accountants are often dealing with complex ideas with many components. Deciding on the order of sentences, and whether to use bullet or numbered lists or other outlining devices, can be a challenge. In the next section, we'll look at a valuable tool for dealing with complex paragraphs. It's called the Christensen Method or Christensen Analysis.

The Christensen Analysis

Let's go back for a moment to the issue of flow. As I mentioned before, when you feel that your writing doesn't flow properly—and sometimes that's just a gut feeling—it's usually a problem with the paragraphs. A sentence can be in the wrong paragraph, or even in the right paragraph but in the wrong order.

What we need is a method of isolating these problem sentences so that we can put them where they belong. Fortunately, we have such a method, thanks to Professor Francis Christensen of the University of California, who developed it back in the mid-sixties.

The Christensen Method helps us analyze paragraphs in a particular way so that a problem sentence, and the reason it is a problem, stand out clearly. Now you'll see in a moment that it's a process. It takes at least a few minutes to complete it, and for that reason I don't for a moment suggest you subject all your paragraphs to the method. It's a diagnostic tool and you use it only when necessary.

For purposes of the Christensen Method, there are two types of paragraph structure:

a) In the subordinate paragraph, each sentence is more specific than the one before, taking the reader deeper into the statement made in the topic sentence. To make sense, the sentences must come in the right order.

b) In the co-ordinate paragraph, each sentence after the topic sentence is at the same level of specificity about the topic and they could logically come in any order.

Here's how the method works.

Christensen assigns a number to each sentence in the paragraph. Number 1 is always the topic sentence which, as we know, introduces the reader to the subject of the paragraph. The other numbers are based on their specific relationship to the topic sentence and the other sentences in the paragraph. The further away from the generality of the topic sentence, and the more specific, the higher the number.

The best way for me to explain this is by showing you, so

here's the first paragraph I'm going to analyze:

> *Most successful accountants have certain personal characteristics. They have a mind and an eye for detail. They can read numbers as others read words. They enjoy the challenge of reading the message of the numbers.*

Now let's separate the sentences and assign Christensen's numbers to them:

1. Most successful accountants have certain personal characteristics.

2. They have a mind and an eye for detail.

2. They can read numbers as others read words.

2. They enjoy the challenge of reading the message of the numbers.

As mentioned, the topic sentence is assigned a 1. In assigning the others, I considered their relationship to the topic sentence and to one another, and I concluded the relationship was the same for all and they could actually appear in any order. That is the definition of a co-ordinate paragraph, and these are usually quite easy to analyze. You are less likely to disrupt the flow too, because you can change the order of the 2. sentences without problem.

Here's another example:

> *For purposes of determining the arm's length royalty for such intangibles, we have considered certain information provided to us by Bolid Software's management. First, a May 15, 2010 report prepared*

> *by another major consultant estimated the total value of the Bolid software to be approximately $321,000. The Rippit software was valued at $207,000. The report noted that Rippit was the company's flagship product.The Plungit software was valued at $95,000. The Squeezit software currently in development was valued at $19,000.*

Let's subject it to the Christensen analysis:

1. For purposes of determining the arm's length royalty for such intangibles, we have considered certain information provided to us by Bolid Software's management.

2. First, a May 15, 2010 report prepared by another major consultant estimated the total value of the Bolid software to be approximately $321,000.

3. The Rippit software was valued at $207,000.

4. The report noted that Rippit was the company's flagship product.

3. The Plungit software was valued at $95,000.

3. The Squeezit software currently in development was valued at $19,000

Note that the second sentence follows logically from the first. The sentences with a 3 all have the same relationship to the second sentence and could be in any order. The sentence with a 4 relates to the previous sentence, but by putting it before the other 3 sentences, we disrupt the flow of the paragraph.

The reason this method helps you maintain flow is that

sentences that are in the wrong place in the paragraph, or that don't belong in the paragraph at all, are immediately obvious.

Let's say, for example, we changed the order of the last paragraph and put the sentence, *The report noted that Rippit was the company's flagship product* before the three 3 sentences. It doesn't make sense, does it? On performing the Christensen analysis, you would immediately recognize the problem with the paragraph flow.

Depending on the context, it might make sense to make the 4. sentence a 1. and use it as the topic sentence for another paragraph.

This process actually takes longer to write about than to do, so please don't be put off trying the method because it sounds complicated. Once you've done it a couple of times you'll be able to identify the levels of the sentences and assign them numbers very quickly. This will put you in command of an excellent tool for creating a written message that flows well and conveys its message easily, without confusion.

Jargon: How to Baffle Clients

Imagine how you'd feel if your lawyer said this:

> *The revocation by these Regulations of a provision previously revoked subject to savings does not affect the continued operation of those savings.*

Or your doctor said this:

> *We could do an FPG test to check your blood glucose, but we've found that the OGTT test is more sensitive so in your case we'll schedule that one. If it turns out you have impaired fasting glucose we'll do the FPG test the following day.*

Or your plumber said this:

> *Your water system is different from your drain and waste plumbing. The water system depends on pressure through the pipes. But with drain and waste there's no pressure except gravity. We just couple the vent piping with the drain and waste to exhaust sewer*

> *gases and equalize the pressure so the drains can drain.*

My guess is you'd either feel stupid because you didn't understand (even though there's no reason why you should) or annoyed at them for baffling you with their jargon. Either way, it wouldn't do much for your professional relationship, would it?

Could you be doing this to your clients? Imagine their reaction when you send them this:

> *A Restricted Share means a phantom share granted, which is equivalent in value and in dividend and interest rights to a Share, and which upon or following vesting entitles the participant to receive a Share or its Fair Market Value in cash. At the discretion of the company, a grant of Restricted Shares may include a tandem Distribution Equivalent Right, allowing a specific Restricted Share to receive an amount in cash equal to the cash distributions made by the company in respect of a Share. The Distribution Equivalent Right can accrue to the participant or be paid to the participant at the time of the cash distribution in respect to a Share.*

If you see no problem with this, just hand it to someone who's not an accountant and watch their eyes roll up in their sockets!

We're All Guilty

We all use jargon, and most of us misuse it at least some of the time even though we may not realize it. The trouble is that we are so accustomed to these words that we don't even think of them as jargon.

In a public workshop I conducted, one woman said the people in her company never used jargon. Intrigued, I asked her what kind of company it was and she said, with a perfectly straight face, "We manufacture plastic extrusion profiles from pre-prototype to post production, and our specialty is high precision tolerances." She seemed quite surprised when most of the others in the group laughed!

When you speak to clients using technical language or jargon, they won't laugh. Nor will they usually ask what you mean, because ironically they think they're supposed to understand. They will, however, probably be baffled. They won't be able to benefit from your valuable professional advice because it will go right over their heads.

Oh yes, they'll nod and thank you and shake your hand as you rise to leave the meeting, but the truth is they are like that cartoon character with the puzzled look on its face and the big question mark over its head!

If they don't understand your advice, they can't follow it. And if they don't follow it, they won't get the right results. And who will they blame? Whose brilliance will be in question? Whose professional reputation will be damaged? I'll let you guess!

Communication Aid or Communication Barrier?

In fact, jargon can be both an aid and a barrier to communication. It all depends on how it's used.

Jargon exists because it helps people communicate through certain words and phrases that describe something these particular people have in common. Under these circumstances, it's an aid to communication. Within your tax practice, for example, your colleagues all know what *transfer pricing, ABIL, capital dividend account* or *yearend rollover* mean. So it makes sense to use the words in professional conversations.

Is it ever OK to use jargon?

Yes, of course. If jargon weren't such a useful form of communication, we wouldn't use it. But the trick is in knowing when it's appropriate and when it's not.

We use jargon as an "in language" among people who understand and use the same words as we do to describe something we all understand. This isn't just in your professional environment; most hobbies and interests have their own words and phrases. This lets us reduce multi-word phrases, for example, to sets of initials or special made-up words, and everyone in the group understands.

But it's important to realize these words *are* jargon, and when you step outside the group that uses this language, you need to consider whether you can take the jargon with you.

In most cases, you need to leave at least part of it behind and use universally understood, plain language terms.

Helen's Jargon Challenge

As I said earlier, often we don't even realize we're using jargon because it's just second nature to us. So it's important to become aware of the words we use, and find a way to communicate without jargon when necessary and appropriate. That's the purpose of Helen's Jargon Challenge.

Using the form below as a starting point, write down as many of your own and your colleagues' jargon terms as you can remember. (You will need to make your own form with much more space because you have more jargon than you think!) Keep the list near you and take a few days to add to it as you think of more words. Now comes the challenge.

For every jargon term in the left column, put in the right column a plain language equivalent word or phrase. Not an explanation, but a translation—a phrase you could actually use in place of the jargon term. Take a shot now at the first few I've put on the list.

Jargon Term	***Plain Language Equivalent***
capital gain	
depreciable property	
impairment of value	
vertical integration	

Now you have a plain language expression for each jargon term: when you speak or write to a non-accountant, use them.

Sometimes the equivalent terms are too long, and you don't want to keep using these phrases all through a written piece. In that case, you can simply define the term the first time you use it and then use the technical term for the rest. This can be done formally, with a Definition of Terms, or by casually explaining the terms in the narrative. Here's what I mean.

Formal

> *Throughout this engagement, we will be following the International Financial Reporting Standards ("IFRS").*

Informal

> *Throughout this engagement, we will be following the International Financial Reporting Standards. We call these IFRS.*

Acronyms

Acronyms and sets of initials are jargon. And by the way, not all sets of initials are technically acronyms. The word acronym originally referred to a set of initials pronounced as a word. Examples would be NATO (North Atlantic Treaty Organization), laser (Light Amplification by Stimulated Emission of Radiation) or, one that needs no explanation for accountants, GAAP (now, of course, going the way of the Tyrranosaurus Rex).

Through usage, we now refer to any sets of initials as acronyms, whether they are pronounced as a word or not. Initials of most professional and trade associations would be examples.

But however you define it, an acronym is jargon, and outside its user group it will create confusion or bafflement.

Picture this. You call the Canadian Society for the Preservation of Groundhog Day and ask to speak to the person who handles the society's financial operations. You are told that would be Arthur Brown. Arthur's not there, so you leave a message on his voicemail asking him to call you.

It turns out Arthur is the wrong person and you need to speak to Betty Robb, but of course you don't know that. So you answer your phone to hear a female voice say, "Hi, this is Betty Robb from CSPGD. How can I help you?" That's a panic-inducing head scratcher, isn't it?

Yes, acronyms are jargon. Use them with care.

Some Final Thoughts on Jargon

Most of what I've said about using jargon in writing also applies in the spoken word. In a conversation with a client, keep your language as free of arcane professional terms as possible. Remember, they won't ask you what you mean because they think they're supposed to know, so you need to take responsibility for being clear.

Three tips:

1. Create your version of Helen's Jargon Challenge, and put it into practice.

2. Ask if you are making yourself clear. Don't ask if they understand because that can sound like a judgement on them. Rather, say something like, "I want to be sure I'm being clear, so is there anything you'd like me to go over again?" Then, find a simpler way to explain what they don't understand.

3. Watch their body language and facial expressions for signs your message is going over their heads. Say it again in a simpler way.

Here's something to ponder. Let's say your team goes in to make a sales presentation to a potential client who is also entertaining proposals from two competitors. Both competitors present a boring, longwinded, jargon-laden explanation of the work to be done. Your team presents exactly the same work, but in terms the client can understand so that it is clear what they can expect. Who do you think is going to get the engagement?

I rest my case. Clear, simple language wins every time.

Grammar: Three Principles You Just Have to Know

This book is a Short Painless Guide, so there's no room in it for an exhaustive (and exhausting!) study of grammar. There are many grammar books and online resources already available (including my own *101 Grammar Gaffes and How to Correct Them*, available for purchase on my website at www.mhwcom.com). So there really is no excuse for grammatically incorrect writing.

There are two main reasons for using correct grammar. First, this is our language, and it's deteriorating because we're not using it well. Learning the grammar and using it properly is one way to reverse this trend.

The other good reason is that when your grammar is wrong, you can actually change the meaning of what you're saying.

For now, I'm going to focus on three grammar principles that you just have to know if your written business communication is not to embarrass you. Rather than delve deep into the grammar rules, I'll illustrate each one by example.

The Apostrophe

The apostrophe has two uses in English: to indicate that the word is a contraction and to form the possessive case.

The first one is simple, so I'll deal with it first.

The words *do not* can be shortened to *don't* simply by using an apostrophe to indicate the missing letter *o*. Similarly, *I am* is shortened to *I'm*, *they are* becomes *they're* and *who is* changes to *who's*. You'll be able to tell from the context whether *he'd* means *he had* or *he would*.

Generally speaking, it's advisable to keep contractions to a minimum in business writing. In a book such as this, however, they help maintain the informal tone I want, and that's why I've used them liberally throughout.

Using the apostrophe to create the possessive can be a little trickier for some. There are just a few rules, though, and if you learn them you'll be able to happily use this useful form, which other languages don't have. Here are the rules:

(a) When a noun does not finish in an *s*, make it possessive by adding *apostrophe s*.

> *the accounts of the company = the company's accounts*
>
> *the fiduciary duty of an accountant = an accountant's fiduciary duty*

Note, this rule applies whether the noun is singular or plural:

> *the dressing room of the men = the men's dressing room*

(b) When a plural noun ends with *s* (as most plural nouns do in English), form the possessive by adding only an apostophe:

> *the accounts of the companies = the companies' accounts*

> *the salaries of the directors = the directors' salaries*

(c) The following is a little trick, rather than a formal grammar rule, but I think you'll find it helpful. When a singular noun ends with *s*, say both words to see if in forming the possessive you add a syllable. If so, form the possessive with *apostrophe s*. If not, form the possessive with just an apostrophe:

> *the office of the boss (boss has one syllable) = the boss's office (boss's has two syllables)*

> *the latest film of the actress (actress has two syllables) = the actress's latest film (actress's has three syllables)*

> *the car of John Saunders (Saunders has two syllables) = John Saunders' car (Saunders' also has two syllables)*

(d) Possessive pronouns, with the single exception of *one's*, do not take an apostrophe:

hers, yours, theirs, his, ours—and ITS!

It's annoyingly common to see the possessive pronoun *its* written incorrectly as *it's*. The only time this word takes an apostrophe is when it's short for *it is*:

everything in its place

it's a difficult problem

That takes care of the apostrophe, but we're not done with the possessive form yet. Now comes the question of how many nouns in a sentence to make possessive.

To indicate joint possession, make only the last noun possessive:

Richard and Janice's business (the business belongs to them both)

Celia is Michael, Tony and Ricardo's mother (Celia "belongs to" all three children)

To indicate individual possession, make all nouns possessive:

the president's and vice-president's reports (each one has a report)

The possessive case can reduce the number of words needed to express a thought clearly. Learn these few rules and use it with confidence.

Subject/Verb Agreement

Subjects and verbs must agree in their number. In other words, singular subjects (including the pronouns *I, you, he, she* or *it*) take singular verbs; plural subjects (including *we, the plural you* or *they*) take plural verbs.

Sounds straighforward and logical, doesn't it? But of course, this is English, so there are complications! Let's discuss them one at a time.

• Sometimes there are words between subject and object, and they can obscure the number:

> *His description of the rules was confusing.* (It's the singular subject *description* that was confusing, not the plural *rules*, so we use the singular verb *was*.)

• When two or more singular subjects are joined with *and*, they become plural and take a plural verb:

> *The business owner and the auditor are collaborating closely.*

• But when singular subjects are joined with words other than *and* (e.g. *as well as, or, nor* etc.) they count as singular and take a singular verb:

> *The lawyer, as well as the accountant, attends the meetings.*

• Collective nouns (group words) usually take a singular verb:

The jury is ready to bring in its verdict.

• But when we are describing actions of individuals within the group, we use the plural verb:

The jury eat their lunch at noon during the trial.

The verdict belongs to the jury as a group, while presumably each juror has his or her own lunch.

• The following indefinite pronouns always take a singular verb:

each, nobody, someone, somebody, everyone, none

The longer and more complex your sentences, the more likely you are to lose the person and number agreement, so check those longer sentences carefully. Where there are singular and plural nouns in the same sentence, the wrong verb number can be at best confusing, and at worst change the meaning of your sentence.

Misplaced and Dangling Modifiers

A modifier is a word that refers to or explains another word in a sentence, and the two should be as close together as possible to avoid confusion. A modifier should not be misplaced or dangling.

Misplaced modifiers

When it's not clear which word the modifier refers to, it's misplaced:

The students cheered as the award winner ran across the stage excitedly.

What was done excitedly—the cheering or the running? It's not clear because the modifier is misplaced. One of the following would correct the sentence:

The students cheered excitedly as the award winner ran across the stage.

The students cheered as the award winner ran excitedly across the stage.

Dangling modifiers

A modifier is dangling when it's not logically connected to anything in the sentence:

Examining the accounts, several inconsistencies were discovered.

As a newly hired auditor, the president welcomed John to the team.

In the first case, who examined the accounts? The inconsistencies? I think not, but that's what the sentence says. In the second case, was the president a newly hired auditor? Probably not. Let's try those again:

When the accounts were examined, several inconsistencies were found.

As a newly hired auditor, John was welcomed to the team by the president.

Misplaced and dangling modifiers can have hilarious results:

> *Here are some tips on handling obscene phone calls from the phone company. (I know, sometimes those calls are obscene.)*

> *Driving down a country lane, a dog suddenly appeared. (Was the dog a good driver?)*

> *While attending an important meeting, my car was stolen. (Maybe you shouldn't have sent your car to the meeting.)*

However, they can also cause serious problems. Consider the following:

> *By paying a premium of 5% of wages, all employees will be included in the policy.*

According to this sentence, who was to pay the 5%? All employees. The problem in this real situation was that it was supposed to be the company, and this sentence was almost a deal breaker. It should have read:

> *By paying a premium of 5% of wages, the company can include all employees in the policy.*

Grammar is important, and I recommend you read some of the many resources to help ensure yours is correct. But at a minimum, make sure you understand these three principles and use them correctly.

Punctuation Without Tears

For the most part, punctuating an English sentence is a matter of logic—although not always; sometimes we just have to memorize not only the rules but also the exceptions.

This template is designed to help you decide what punctuation is appropriate and where to put it without struggling through dozens of grammatical rules. Instead, study the examples below until you're sure you understand them. Then, next time you're not sure how to punctuate a sentence, hold it against the template, find the example with the same construction as your sentence—and simply drop in the punctuation marks. How useful is that?

The template consists of eight sentence constructions in which you need to make a punctuation decision. The seven 'connectors' *for, and, yet, so, nor, or, but* often need specific punctuation. To help you remember these, I refer to them by their initials, FAYSNOB (if you can't remember this cute acronym, just think of your nose!)

The symbol ▼ indicates the place where you must make a punctuation decision, and the correct decision is explained after each.

1. Item (word, phrase or sentence) ▼ item ▼ FAYSNOB item

Cold, tired yet happy

I want to sing, I need to sing and I will sing.

I'm defining an item in this example as a word, a phrase or even a whole sentence. You need commas between the first two but no punctuation before or after the FAYSNOB, in these cases *yet* and *and.*

There's always some question about whether there should be a comma before the final *and*, and in fact there can be a variation in usage between different countries. I follow the convention that says the FAYSNOB takes the place of the final comma, and that's how we know we've reached the end of the list.

The exception is when the last or second last item *contains* a FAYSNOB and we need a comma for clarity.

My favourite foods are bread, cheese, bananas, and fish and chips.

I want *fish and chips* to be read as one item, and the comma makes that clear.

2. Introduction ▼ sentence

After a three-month audit, we had to tell the client he was in trouble.

This week we had to tell the client he was in trouble.

When you place an introductory phrase in front of a complete sentence, you need to put a comma after the introduction.

Note, however, that the second example has no comma. That's because North American Business Standards let you omit the comma when the introduction is short, such as one or two words. The traditional British form still insists on the comma. (Some people will argue to the death over this comma. Both are correct, so don't waste your energy.)

3. Sentence ▼ explanation.

We realized the client was in trouble when we finished the audit.

When we put the complete sentence first, the descriptive information is, of course, no longer an introduction but an explanation. In this case, we need no punctuation between the two parts of the sentence.

4. Sen ▼ interruption with extra information ▼ tence.

The members, who had voted for John as President, were pleased with the result.

But note:

The members who had voted for John as President were pleased with the result.

You really need to understand this one, because by inserting or omitting the commas, you actually change the meaning of the sentence. Here's how it works.

If you put commas around the interrupting phrase *who had voted for John as President,* that means it is extra information about the subject of the sentence (the members) and if you remove it you will still be left with the essence of the meaning, i.e. *The members were pleased with the result.* Clearly, we're talking about all the members.

However, when we omit the commas, as in the second example, the phrase is no longer extra information but defining information. Not all the members were pleased with the result—just the ones who had voted for John as President. Big difference.

Read this a few times and try it out with your own sentences to be sure you understand it. You don't want to risk saying the wrong thing because you made the wrong choice about the commas!

5. Sentence ▼ FAYSNOB ▼ sentence.

The Chairman stood up, and he made a great speech.

The Chairman stood up and made a great speech.

This is one that usually makes me stop to think, because really I can't for the life of me see that it makes any difference —at least in terms of meaning. But we might as well get it right, so here it is.

When you join two complete sentences together with a FAYSNOB, you need a comma before the FAYSNOB and no punctuation after it. As you can see, each of the two parts of the first example is a complete sentence by itself. But if you look at the second example, you'll see that the part of the sentence after the FAYSNOB (*and*) is not a complete sentence; so in this case, we don't need any punctuation at all.

6. Punctuated sentence ▼ FAYSNOB ▼ Punctuated sentence

> *The manager, feeling pleased with herself, presented the budget. The vice-president, who had different priorities, would not approve it.*

Use a FAYSNOB to join these sentences, which already contain punctuation, as follows:

> *The manager, feeling pleased with herself, presented the budget; but the vice-president, who had different priorities, would not approve it.*

Another example:

> *After many years of trying, I won the lottery; but although I thought it would make me happy, it did not.*

Much of the way we construct sentences is intuitive, and it's based on the way we speak—with the result that sometimes we great quite long sentences. There's nothing wrong with a long sentence, as long as it's understandable.

In these examples we've taken two sentences that have already been punctuated using one of the other constructions and joined them using a FAYSNOB. We need punctuation before the FAYSNOB, but if we just put a comma here it would be added to all the other commas and just create confusion. We need more than a comma; we need a semi-colon.

7. Sentence ▼ sentence

> *We must always remember our first rule: the customer is always right.*

I love this construction. It's a very elegant way of joining two complete sentences without adding any words, but instead by using a colon. The trick here is that the second sentence has to depend on the first sentence for its meaning. So in our example, *the customer is always right* IS the first rule.

Never use a comma here. That would create a run-on sentence, the second most common grammatical error in business writing. (The most common is writing a fragment instead of a complete sentence.)

8. Sentence ▼ transitional marker other than FAYSNOB ▼ sentence

> *He had a prior appointment; therefore, he did not attend the meeting.*

> *We appreciate all applications; however, we only acknowledge those under consideration.*

This is another of the most common grammatical mistakes in written English. When you join two complete sentences using a transitional word that is not a FAYSNOB (e.g. *however, therefore*), you need a semi-colon before the transitional word and a comma after it. Carefully read the two examples and you'll see what I mean.

Many people think you always have to put commas around *however*, but that's not correct. I could say,

> *We only, however, acknowledge those under consideration.*

Can you spot the difference? In this example the parts around the *however* are not complete sentences, so the comma is enough. But in the first two examples, they are complete sentences, so we need that semi-colon.

So there you have eight examples to help you decide what the correct punctuation mark is and where to put it. Keep it close to you, use it well and you'll never again suffer from punctuation perplexity!

Email: the Particular Writing Challenges

In very broad terms, people make two basic mistakes in writing email: too longwinded and too terse—opposite ends of the spectrum when it comes to conveying information. Both lead to less-than-effective communication.

Email has somehow never really claimed its proper place in our written communication at work. Oh we use it all the time, but it's still the poor relation of the formal written message. The result is that we don't give it enough thought, enough attention, enough respect. We dash off words carelessly and hit the 'send' button, often without even reading what we've written.

Let's look at some principles that will make our business email the effective, time-saving medium it was always meant to be.

Get to the Point Quickly

> *With respect to the question of whether or not Client X must charge retail sales tax on the materials required to produce the bamboo flooring he sells to his clients, it is necessary to differentiate between those clients for whom he installs the flooring and those to whom he merely sells the materials.*

Whew! 53 words! That's a very long opening sentence, and unfortunately it's not an unusual one. In the old days of printed letters and memos, you might have been able to get away with this, but today's reader is way too impatient to wade through all those words. It's just too easy to hit the delete button if we are not immediately drawn into the message, and unfortunately that's what happens to a lot of legitimate email.

You have two chances to grab your reader's attention and persuade him or her to read your email: the subject line and the opening sentence. I'll deal with the subject line in a moment, but first—look again at that opening sentence. The one with 53 words!

Not only are there too many words, but they don't trip easily off the tongue, do they? I can't imagine anyone actually saying this out loud, and that's often a good test of whether words are appropriate. That makes it even more difficult for readers to absorb the information, and even more likely they won't bother trying.

Some of us write this way naturally, and if that lets you get the words down on the page or up on the screen that's fine. Just remember to treat it as a draft and edit it before you send it out. In editing, ask yourself what is the core of what you're trying to say. In this case, it's the difference in tax treatment between selling a product and selling a service. So let's take another shot at actually saying that:

> *Whether or not Client X must charge retail sales tax to his flooring customers depends on whether he is selling and installing the flooring, or merely selling the materials for the flooring.*

At 31 words it's still a long sentence, but there's no fluff here. By the time the reader reaches the end of the first sentence, it will be clear what the email is about.

Have you ever been to the theatre? You know that moment when the curtains open, and even if there's nobody onstage the scenery sets the scene for you? Well that's what the opening sentence of your email must do for your reader. Don't bury the message under a pile of useless words.

Give the Message Structure

It seems to be the nature of email that we don't do much planning before we start to write the message. Judging by many email messages I've read, it seems many folks just sit down and start typing, and it all comes out in a stream-of-consciousness jumble of words. They don't express their thoughts in a logical order, but just as they pop into their heads. The reader is left trying to follow a message that jumps all over the place instead of flowing logically and easily from a beginning to an end.

As I said when I was discussing the opening sentence, if this helps you to get your thoughts down, that's fine. But just remember you can't send it out like that! Treat it as a draft that must be carefully read and edited before you hit the 'send' button.

Here's a simple structure for an effective email that suits most subjects and circumstances:

- Opening: your reason for writing
- Body of message expressed point by point
- Close, including call to action if appropriate

Make Your Subject Line Do Its Job

How much email comes into your emailbox in the average day? More than you want, I'll bet. And of course the same is true for everyone else. That's why most of us spend at least some time every day whizzing through the subject lines on those emails and making that decision: delete, delete, delete.

Your email's first defence against deletion is the subject line.

What's the job of the subject line? To make the reader read the message. If your subject line doesn't do its job your email might well hit the trash without even being read.

There are two principles to bear in mind when writing an effective subject line:

- Make it specific
- Make it address the reader's interests

You might send me an email with the subject line, *Client X Audit Planning Meeting*. I happen to know this meeting is scheduled for one month from now. I have lots of time to prepare for it, and I have many more pressing things to attend to. So even though I don't actually delete the message, I decide to leave it for now and read it later. Well you know what that means, don't you? It gets buried among all those other emails that just keep coming, and eventually I may inadvertently delete it unread. And that could be serious, because you were writing to tell me the meeting had been moved forward by ten days.

But let's say you use a different subject line: *Change in date of Client X Audit Planning Meeting (urgent)*

That's quite different, isn't it? Now it's in my interests to read the message because I want to know what's changed. That very specific subject line will have a much more positive result than the first more general one because it meets both criteria I mentioned above.

Email is just a medium. It's a substitute for ink on paper, not for the message itself or the need to write it correctly and well. So when the message is substantive, we need to put as much effort into writing it as we would a message intended for the printed page.

Report Writing the DESIGN IT™ Way

I've called this process report writing, but I'm using the words in a generic sense, because it can be used to write any piece that is longer than a page or so. So besides pieces that are actually called reports, such as audit reports, you can use the process for client reporting letters, opinion letters or other longer written messages.

Many years ago, a young lawyer told me he was concerned that he wrote too many drafts, and when he told me he averaged seven or eight for one message, I had to agree with him! His problem was a common one though, and not only among lawyers. He would start writing a long written message by—well—writing it! He didn't give any thought to planning how best to present his message, or what his purpose was. He just started writing.

Imagine you were driving to a city far away from your own, one you'd never visited before. Wouldn't you consult a map? Most people would not only look at the map, but choose the best route and plan milestones along the way. If you don't do this, you're likely to have many false starts, wrong turnings and a journey much longer than it need be.

That's what happens when you start writing a longer piece without a plan. In this section, I'm going to explain the method I call DESIGN IT™.

DESIGN IT™ is an acronym for the eight steps in the process, which are as follows:

- **D**ecide what to include
- **E**ach topic has its own section
- **S**top gaps and eliminate duplication
- **I**ntroduce headings
- **G**et it in order
- **N**ow write the first draft
- **I**nterval: get distance from the first draft
- **T**ransform it through editing

This is a low tech method, and that sometimes takes people aback when I first discuss it. However, I believe the low tech approach in this instance has advantages over doing it all on your computer, and I'll point those out as I come to them in the example that follows.

I also want to point out that it takes much longer for me to explain this method than it will actually take you to use it, so don't let the length of this section discourage you. Even if you are skeptical, I urge you to keep it in reserve, and next time you're stuck, facing writer's block, give it a spin. You'll be pleasantly surprised.

To illustrate the DESIGN IT™ process, I need to have a sample to work on. Rather than focusing too closely on the actual content, I want you to clearly see and understand the process. So I'm not going to use an accounting sample, but rather a more general business scenario.

Imagine you have been leading a project team to investigate starting a knowledge management program at your firm or company. You've done the work, and now you must write the report to management, with your recommendations. Let's use the DESIGN IT™ method to plan and write this report.

D: Decide What to Include

When you are writing a longer piece, you'll often be working from a fat file of information you've been accumulating for the purpose—especially if it's a client reporting letter you've been avoiding for months! Some of this material will be included in the report, while some is just background and won't be used. The first task, then, is to decide what to include.

For this, you'll need a pad (or several) of Post It™ notes. Yes, yes, I know—I did warn you this was a low tech method. I also promised to explain my reasons at the right time and we haven't reached that yet, so stay cool for now.

Here's how you'll use the Post It™ notes (I like to call them yellow stickies, partly because it saves me having to type in the ™ every time and partly because that's what I call them when I speak.) Anyway, whatever you choose to call them, have a pad at the ready and start going through the papers in your file.

Each time you see a topic you want to include in your report, jot down a few key words on a yellow sticky to remind you what it is, and turn that sheet over. Don't separate the sheets just now. Keep doing this until you have reviewed the whole file. If you think of anything else that's not in the file, jot that down too.

Depending on how much material there is, you'll have one or more pads of yellow stickies with key words jotted down on them all. And that completes the *D* step.

E: Each Topic Has Its Own Section

The next low tech item you'll need is an ordinary lined pad or a bunch of typing paper. You'll use a number of these sheets to separate the information into topics, each of which will have its own section. Here's how you'll do that.

Go through your yellow sticky notes and, reading the keywords on each, separate them by topic. Each new topic you recognize will be stuck on a new lined sheet. This keeps your notes semi-organized, so if you are interrupted in the middle of the task to take care of something else (as if that would ever happen to you!) it's easy to gather them up and then spread them out again when you resume.

At the end of this stage, you'll have several sheets, each of which will be host to a number of sticky notes on a particular aspect of your report. Going back to our example of the report on the proposed knowledge management program, your topic list might look something like this:

> The need for a central repository for all the company's knowledge
>
> Who has this knowledge now and how can we find it?
>
> Getting people's help in identifying their knowledge
>
> The technology platform
>
> Develop the information management process, roles and responsibilities
>
> Set expectations and objectives for the program
>
> Educate employees on importance of program and their contribution
>
> Start with pilot
>
> Measuring the results

In this case, you would have nine sheets representing the nine topics.

And that completes the "E" step.

S: Stop Gaps and Eliminate Duplication

Have you ever written something on page five of a report and suddenly thought it sounded eerily familiar—and it turned out you had already covered this topic on page two?

Or have you ever finished your first draft, only to realize you had completely missed out a topic?

If you follow the DESIGN IT™ process well, this won't happen because you'll be able to see gaps and duplication at this stage. Here's how.

Spread all your sheets out in front of you and carefully look at all the yellow stickies. You might find one or all of the following:

1. Topics that appear in more than one section, perhaps under slightly different words but essentially the same.
2. Topics you had forgotten until you saw all this content in front of you.
3. Topics that are on the wrong sheet, and therefore destined to appear in the wrong section of the report.

Correct them thus:

1. Decide where the topic does belong and remove the stickies from the other sheet.
2. Decide which section the topic belongs in, write the yellow sticky note and put it in the appropriate place.
3. Move the sticky notes to the right section.

This is the first advantage of the low tech approach. Of course you could type all your topics on your computer instead of yellow stickies, but you couldn't see them all without scrolling through. So you wouldn't have this opportunity to easily see gaps and duplication. Score one for low tech!

Now you've completed the *S* part, and your material is beginning to have some semblance of organized information instead of just piles of raw data.

I: Introduce Headings

Imagine how difficult it would be to read a long newspaper or magazine article that had no headings. The headings are there to help the reader through the subject matter, and you should use them in the same way for your reports and longer written materials. Accountants often forget this useful communication device.

That's why the next step in DESIGN IT™ is Introduce Headings. At this point, I'm concerned only with major headings. Your report may well need another level of sub-headings, but don't worry about those for now. If you do need them, that will become apparent when you've written your first draft.

For now, simply spread out your sheets and write a heading on each one. You might consider editing the headings later to make them more meaningful, but for now you can choose generic headings just to get them written.

And that's it for this section. We're really moving along now, aren't we?

G: Get It In Order

At this point you have a collection of sheets, each with notes for one topic section, but you don't want to put them in just any old order. Based on the report purpose and content, you need to decide which topic comes first, second, etc.

There's a psychological principle known as the Law of Primacy and Recency. That just means people remember best what they read first and what they read last. Those are the points when your reader's attention is at its peak, so don't waste them droning on about things he or she already knows.

A great rule of thumb for longer written pieces is this: start with your conclusion. Why? Because everything you write after that will act as support or evidence for your conclusion. If it's what the reader expected and wanted, she may not even read the rest at that time as you'll have validated her opinion in your first sentence. On the other hand, if your conclusion comes as a surprise, she'll have to read your report to find out why you reached it. Either way, starting with the conclusion focuses the reader's attention.

In fashioning your ending, follow the principles of the advertising world and end with a call to action. If you're selling something, ask for the order. If you're providing information, invite the reader to call you with any questions. If you're looking for a budget increase, ask for it.

Finally, organize the rest of the information in the most logical way, and you've finished with "G".

N: Now Write the First Draft

You may have noticed that we've now completed five of the

steps, and we haven't written a word yet. Until you've tried this method, you may be a bit frustrated by this. But I urge you to withhold judgement for now, because all this time spent on preparation will mean the actual writing will go much more quickly and smoothly, and the end product will be of a much higher quality.

The purpose of the first draft is to get the words down on paper—yes, on paper, not just up on the screen. I'll explain why in a moment. At this stage it's not about well written sentences or just the right words. That will come later when you edit your work.

And that brings me to a very important principle: don't edit as you write. I'll say that again: don't edit as you write. Editing your work as you go along is an exercise in frustration, because it will take you much longer to complete the draft. Writing and editing are two separate processes, and they shouldn't be mixed. (I'll have more to say about editing later.)

Writing the DESIGN IT™ Draft

This is where the low tech approach really comes into its own, and I love seeing how quickly I can write my first draft this way. Here's how it works.

Choose which section you'll write first. That doesn't necessarily mean the section that will come first in the final piece—you can write that last if you like. In fact, you can write the sections in any order you like, so why not start with the easiest one?

Put that sheet in front of you. Looking at all the yellow stickies on the sheet, choose the one you'll address first, and write the corresponding sentence or sentences. When that's done, take that yellow sticky off the sheet and throw it away. Then choose the next one, write it and throw away the sticky. Keep repeating these steps until the section is done.

How will you know it's done? There won't be any yellow stickies left on the sheet! As long as there's a note on the sheet, you have more to write; when the sheet is empty, you've finished. Pat yourself on the back and move on to the next section, following the same steps.

Let me demonstrate, using the knowledge management report. I'm going to draft the section on choosing the technology. On the next page is a drawing of my section sheet covered with yellow stickies. To simulate the process, I'll choose a key word, write the sentence or sentences and then show the drawing with that sticky removed, and repeat until the sheet is empty.

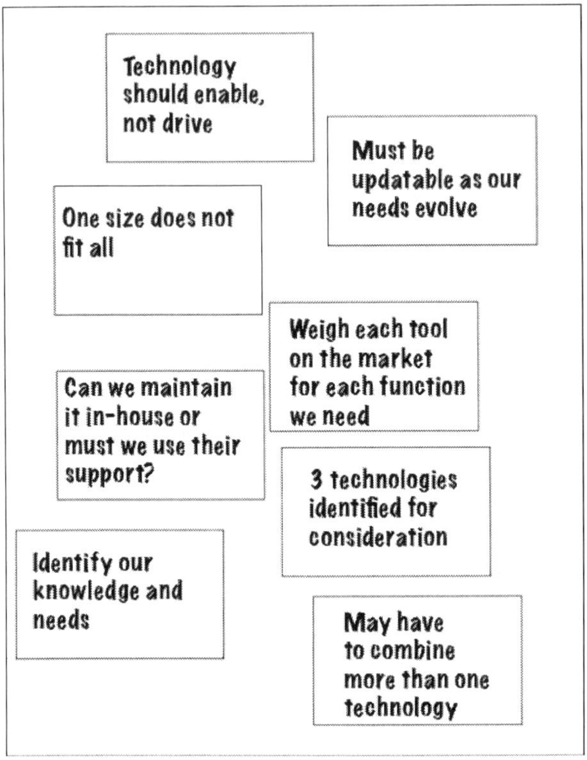

Here's what I wrote based on the first yellow sticky:

> *There is a large and growing selection of knowledge management technology on the market, but it's important to begin with an understanding of our business purpose for the program. The technology should not drive the program, but rather serve and support our purpose for the program.*

Remove that sticky and now the sheet looks like this:

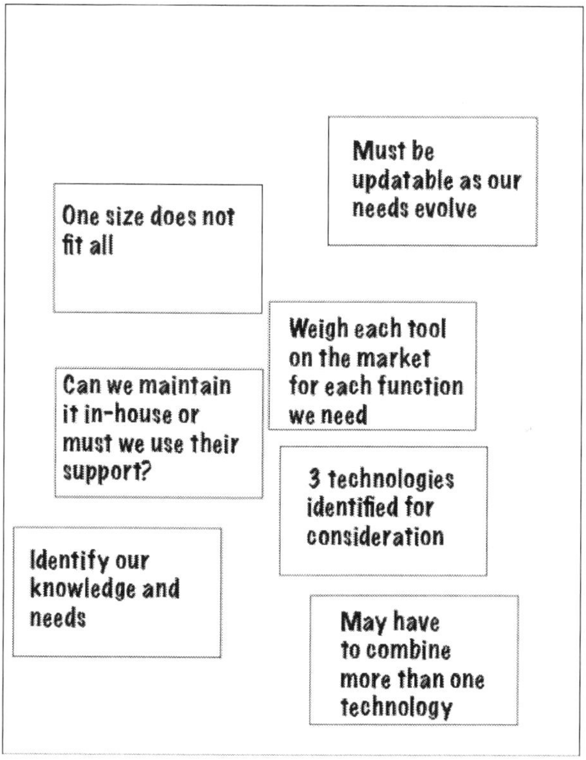

Sometimes you'll find two stickies address the same topic and can be linked, and that's what I've done next:

> *Choosing our knowledge management technology is not a one-size-fits-all situation. The size of our organization, the business we are in, the age of the organization, the number of people and the amount of existing knowledge will all be factors in our choice. It is even possible that we will have to choose more than one technology to get the right combination of functions.*

This leaves the sheet looking like this.

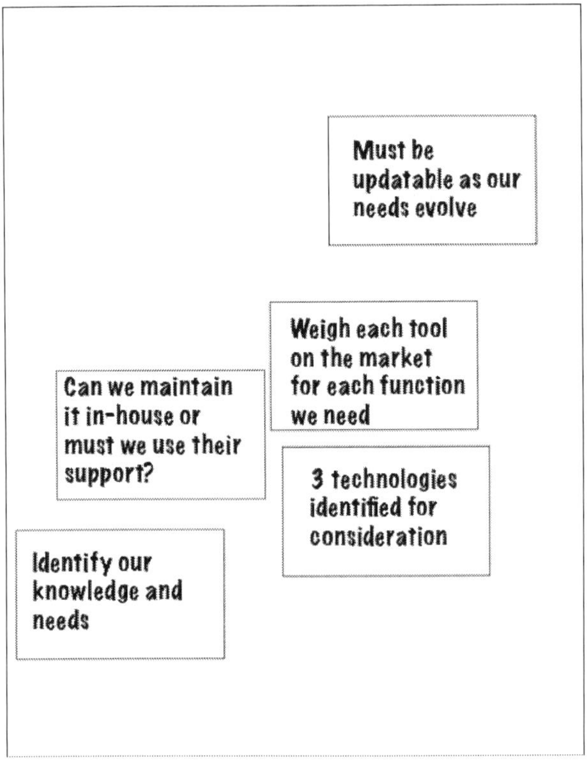

Once again I addressed two of the stickies together for the next part:

> *We must begin by identifying the functions, tools and types of information we will be gathering and sorting, and any special needs created by them. Then we will need to weigh each technology against each one, perhaps giving them a score. This will give us a mathematical picture of them all to help us choose.*

Now we have just three left. This is going well, isn't it?

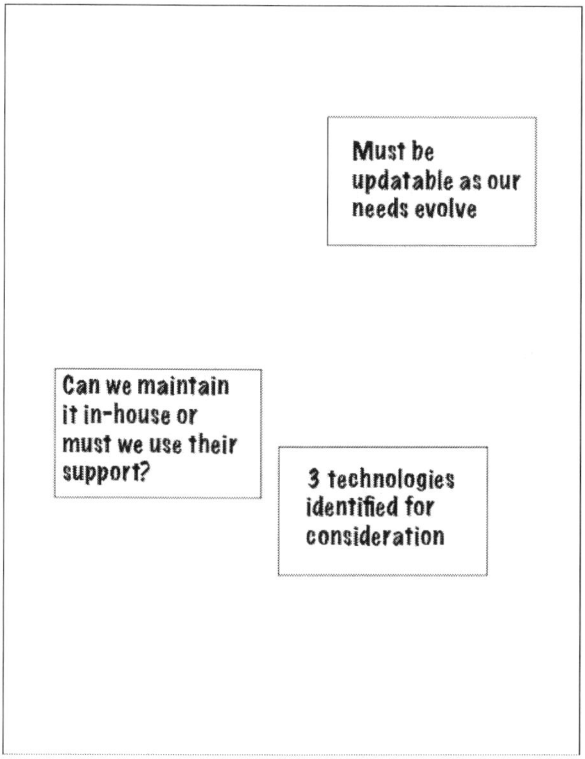

After examining many available technologies, we have identified three we feel are worth close examination for our purposes. They are: Acme, Bolid and Turnpike.

Only two stickies left now, and I think we can combine them again.

> *The technology we choose must be capable of update as our needs evolve. It's also important that we can do much of the maintenance in-house and not have to rely on the technology supplier for all our support needs. If our knowledge management program is to succeed, the choice of technology is paramount.*

Look, Mom—no stickies!

That means we have written all we need to write for this

section, at least in the first draft. When we join the pieces together, we have the draft of the technology section.

> *There is a large and growing selection of knowledge management technology on the market, but it is important to begin with an understanding of our business purpose for the program. The technology should not drive the program, but rather serve and support our purpose for the program. Choosing our knowledge management technology is not a one-size-fits-all situation. The size of our organization, the business we are in, the age of the organization, the number of people and the amount of existing knowledge will all be factors in our choice. It is even possible that we will have to choose more than one technology to get the right combination of functions. We must begin by identifying the functions, tools and types of information we will be gathering and sorting, and any special needs created by them. Then we will need to weigh each technology against each one, perhaps giving them a score. This will give us a mathematical picture of them all to help us choose. After examining many available technologies, we have identified three we feel are worth close examination for our purposes. They are: Acme, Bolid and Turnpike. The technology we choose must be capable of update as our needs evolve. It is also important that we can do much of the maintenance in-house and not have to rely on the technology supplier for all our support needs. If our knowledge management program is to succeed, the choice of technology is paramount.*

Perfect, right? Wrong! It needs a lot of help before it's ready for its readers. But then that's the purpose of a first draft—to get the words and ideas on paper. So all we have to do now is follow the same process for each section and our first draft will be done.

People often tell me that facing the blank screen, trying to get the first draft started, is a major challenge for them. That's because they haven't organized their ideas, but when you use the DESIGN IT™ process, that part takes care of itself!

Now let's move on to the next step.

I: Interval—Get Distance from the First Draft

It's very tempting to start editing your draft as soon as it's finished, but resist. Instead, print it, put it aside for a while and do something else.

Why? Because if you start editing right away you'll be approaching it with the same mindset as you had when you wrote it, and you won't clearly see the parts that could be improved or that really need to be changed. On the other hand, when you come back to it after thinking about other things for a couple of hours, it's almost like having a second opinion.

If you can, leave it until the next day before editing. If you don't have that luxury, take whatever time you can, even if it means just having a coffee and making a couple of phone calls.

I've often had the experience of looking at something I've written a few days before and hardly recognizing it—I actually don't remember writing those words! That frees my mind to look at it from other angles, which usually results in better editing.

So now it's a day later and you're ready for the final step.

T: Transform It through Editing

I emphasized earlier that you should not write and edit at the same time, because they are two separate processes needing different types of thinking. In the writing phase you are using your creativity to get your ideas down on paper. Now that you are ready to edit, you need to put on your analytical hat, focus on the ideas behind the words and ensure those ideas are expressed in the most effective way.

A common mistake in editing is to simply start at line one and plod through all the details of every sentence. Not only is that mind numbing, but it's also ineffective. A much better approach is to go through the material several times, looking at a different aspect each time. In doing this, follow the inverted triangle below:

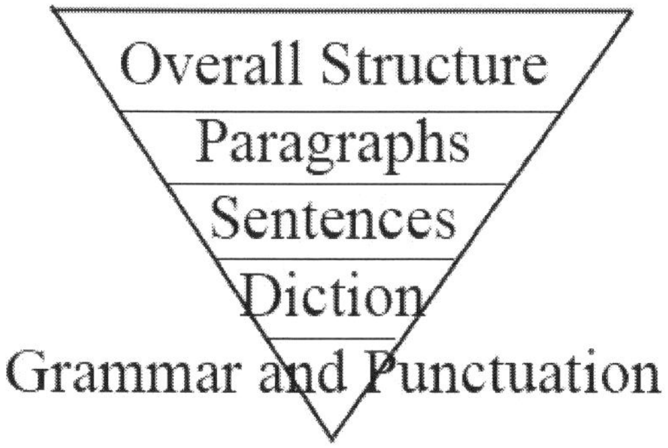

Overall Structure

Begin with the big picture. Examine the overall structure of the message to ensure it is in the right order, and the ideas flow logically from one to the other.

A quick look at the headings will tell you whether they are in the best order. It might have seemed so when you were writing the draft, but sometimes a second look opens up other possibilities, and a couple of changes might make the piece more effective.

At this point it might also become apparent that some of the sections naturally break into other, smaller sections. If that's the case, sub-headings might be helpful to the reader.

This step doesn't usually take very long, but it can make a big difference to the impact of your report.

Paragraphs

Have you written power paragraphs with focus, unity and coherence? Do they read easily and logically? Is the flow right?

At this stage you might get that feeling of unease that says something just doesn't flow the way it should. If that's the case, it might be time to try the Christensen Analysis. It's a great tool for diagnosing misplaced sentences that interfere with the smooth movement of the writing.

Sentences

As I said earlier, sentences are the engine of the written

message, and if you have those right you are moving in the right direction.

Have you written power sentences using predominantly the active voice, action verbs and specific words? Have you kept the core of the sentences together, or spread them throughout a long sentence, resulting in a convoluted message that needs several readings before it makes sense? Remember, if they have to read it twice they probably won't, so straighten out all those convolutions.

Look closely at the emphasis you've created in your sentences through the use of transitional words and phrases as well as the co-ordinate or subordinate relationship between the clauses. If there's room for misunderstanding, massage the words until it's cleared up.

Diction

Used in this sense, the word *diction* refers to word choice.

Have you used words that your reader can reasonably expect to understand, or is your message full of jargon that may shut the reader out?

Have you used the right word in the right place, or is your credibility in jeopardy because you said *pour* when you meant *pore*? If you are unsure about the meaning of a word, check the dictionary. If you're still not sure, find a different word—there are thousands available.

Is your reader drowning in a sea of complicated words? Remember, even if people do understand them individually, their eyes are likely to glaze over when confronted with many fancy words in a row. I'm not suggesting you write at kindergarten level, but simplify at least some of the words to give your reader's mind a break.

Grammar and Punctuation

You may be tempted to begin with a review of grammar and punctuation, but it makes more sense to leave it for last step. That's because in the course of the first couple of reviews you may well take out chunks of the text, and it seems a shame to spend time on the commas and then throw it out anyway.

Far be it from me to assume your grammar skills are poor, because I realize many readers know their grammar as well as I do. But for others that's not the case. If you are working on your grammar, it will improve with practice, and the day may come when you don't need the final review because you'll instinctively do it as you go along.

However, assuming you do the review, use the information in the grammar section of this book as a guide. If you want to go deeper, invest in a grammar resource such as Strunk & White's *Elements of Style* or even my own *101 Grammar Gaffes and How to Correct Them.*

Refer to *Punctuation Without Tears* in the grammar section if you are in doubt about where a comma goes, or whether a comma or other punctuation mark is called for.

If you subject your draft to this rigorous editing process, you will improve it dramatically. Remember, good editing always improves good writing.

So let's use the process on my first draft of the technology section of the report on knowledge management. Again, here's what I wrote:

> *There is a large and growing selection of knowledge management technology on the market, but it's important to begin with an understanding of our business purpose for the program. The technology should not drive the program, but rather serve and support our purpose for the program. Choosing our knowledge management technology is not a one-size-fits-all situation. The size of our organization, the business we are in, the age of the organization, the number of people and the amount of existing knowledge will all be factors in our choice. It is even possible that we will have to choose more than one technology to get the right combination of functions. We must begin by identifying the functions, tools and types of information we will be gathering and sorting, and any special needs created by them. Then we will need to weigh each technology against each one, perhaps giving them a score. This will give us a mathematical picture of them all to help us choose. After examining many available technologies, we have identified three we feel are worth close examination for our purposes. They are: Acme, Bolid and Turnpike. The technology we choose must be capable of update as our needs evolve. It is also important that we can do much of the maintenance in-house and not have to rely on the technology*

> *supplier for all our support needs. If our knowledge management program is to succeed, the choice of technology is paramount.*

Overall Structure

Of course, this is just one section of the report, but it's still a good idea to start with the big picture. A quick look at this tells me it needs to be broken into several paragraphs. Remember: one topic, one paragraph.

If our knowledge management program is to succeed, the choice of technology is paramount. There is a large and growing selection of knowledge management technology on the market, but it's important to begin with an understanding of our business purpose for the program. The technology should not drive the program, but rather serve and support our purpose for the program.

> *Choosing our knowledge management technology is not a one-size-fits-all situation. The size of our organization, the business we are in, the age of the organization, the number of people and the amount of existing knowledge will all be factors in our choice. It is even possible that we will have to choose more than one technology to get the right combination of functions.*
>
> *We must begin by identifying the functions, tools and types of information we will be gathering and sorting, and any special needs created by them. Then we will need to weigh each technology against each*

> *one, perhaps giving them a score. This will give us a mathematical picture of them all to help us choose.*
>
> *The technology we choose must be capable of update as our needs evolve. It is also important that we can do much of the maintenance in-house and not have to rely on the technology supplier for all our support needs.*
>
> *After examining many available technologies, we have identified three we feel are worth close examination for our purposes. They are Acme, Bolid and Turnpike.*

This step clarified the flow of the message for me, and I realized the last three ideas were in the wrong order. I've moved the last sentence of the draft to the beginning and ended with the paragraph about the three technologies identified. Do you agree?

Paragraphs

I think I've done a pretty good job on the paragraphs, as each one has a clear topic sentence supported by others on the same topic.

Sentences

This is the part of the editing process I really enjoy. My editing philosophy is simple: *slash and burn*! I can cut away needless fluff, extra words and redundant phrases. I can twist the sentences around so that they convey my message more clearly and persuasively.

In the process of editing your sentences, sometimes your paragraphs will also change, as you'll see from the next version below.

> *The right choice of technology is essential for the success of our knowledge management program. Despite the large and growing selection of KM technology on the market, we must not allow the technology to be the driver. Rather, it must support our business purposes.*
>
> *No one KM solution fits all organizations. The size, type, and age of our company, as well as the amount and type of knowledge our people have, will be factors in our choice. We may even need a combination of technologies.*
>
> *We must begin by identifying the functions, tools, and types of information we will gather and sort, and any special needs they create. We will then weigh each technology against each need and assign them a score. This statistical analysis will help us make an informed choice of technology.*
>
> *Our KM needs will evolve with time, and we must be able to update the technology as appropriate. We must also be able to maintain the system in-house rather than relying on supplier support.*
>
> *Of the many technologies we have examined, we have*

identified three as worth considering: Acme, Bolid and Turnpike.

Diction

I have avoided using jargon in this case—which was quite easy, as I'm not a knowledge management expert! As you've seen, however, I did shorten the term to KM after the first use. I'm assuming the person who asked me to do this study will understand what the letters mean, and I may even have included them in a definition of terms earlier in the report.

Grammar and Punctuation

I checked to be sure I followed the punctuation and grammar rules as I know them, and I'm confident in the result.

In the real world, this step might take longer and go into more detail. That depends on the situation. However, in this editing exercise I've reduced the word count from 239 to 185, and I believe the process has dramatically improved the clarity and impact of the text. Would you agree?

Self-editing is not easy, as we often fall in love with our precious prose (guilty as charged). However, as good editing always improves good writing, it's a worthwhile skill to develop.

When you see the DESIGN IT™ process set out step by step like this, it may look more complicated than it really is, and I hope you won't be discouraged by that. If you don't feel like diving in and trying it right away, I do urge you at least to keep it in mind. Next time you are stuck, suffering from writer's block with a deadline looming for your report, give it a try. You'll never look back!

Editing for Impact

Editing your own writing can be a challenge, because you are so familiar with your own style that you may not easily see how it can be improved. Your favourite words and phrases come so naturally to you that you may not notice how you overwork them, which reduces their effectiveness over time. The same applies to inappropriate use of jargon.

There is a full discussion of the editing process in the section on report writing. In this section, though, let's zero in on a few paragraphs that could benefit from tightening up. I'll first give you a paragraph based on real examples. Next, I'll comment on what's wrong with it, or at least could be improved. Finally, I'll give you my rewrite.

Of course, most messages can be written in several ways, so don't take my version as the only right one. It's just one way to improve this particular message. That said, on with the show.

Sample 1

> *You requested that we address the question of whether or not you are allowed to buy out the shares of Mopal Widgets owned by Bob Sloan outright and whether this can be achieved as part of the amalgamation process. Technically, there is no provision in the amalgamation process that allows for the buyout of one of the shareholders. In fact, it is one of the prerequisites to the application of the amalgamation provisions that all of the shareholders who owned shares of the capital stock of any predecessor corporation immediately before amalgamation receive shares of the capital stock of the amalgamated corporation. It is, however, possible for you to acquire Bob's shares prior to the amalgamation if you prefer for him not to have any ownership in the new corporation. In order to keep the amalgamation process free of this complication, it is recommended that you take that route, for which there are two options available.*

Comments

This message deals with three different aspects of the topic, which means there should be at least three paragraphs.

The writer has fallen into the common traps of having too many words and very complicated sentences.

Rewrite

> *You asked if you were allowed to buy out Bob Sloan's*

shares in Mopal Widgets as part of the amalgamation process.

A prerequisite to the process is that anyone who owns shares of any of the predecessor corporations immediately before amalgamation must receive shares in the amalgamated corporation. A buyout of Bob's shares cannot, therefore, be part of the amalgamation process.

If you do not want Bob to have ownership in the new corporation, however, it is possible for you to acquire his shares before the amalgamation. There are two options for achieving this.

Sample 2

Although we have been able to support the 2010 operating loss using a multi-year analysis, we do not believe it would be possible for us to adequately support the 2011 results on the basis of the current pricing and budget projections. It is the generally accepted principle that for the purposes of transfer pricing a company with limited risks (such as, for example, Bolid Manufacturing) should realize a net profit. Although it is entirely possible that unplanned losses might result from unforeseen events and circumstances, it is not likely that a planned loss could be supported. The fact that Bolid Manufacturing currently projects an operating loss of 7.3% it is to be expected that the Canada Revenue Agency would claim that its prices are not arm's length. Transfer prices would likely be adjusted and penalties are also possible.

Comments

This sample also deals with more than one aspect of the topic. First, there's the statement that the 2011 budget is making it difficult to support the results. Then there's the statement of the regulation that causes the problem. Finally, there's the statement of what this means to the client. Three topics: three paragraphs.

Again, too many unnecessary words are getting in the way of a clear message. Get rid of them—slash and burn!

Rewrite

Although we can support the 2010 operating loss using a multi-year analysis, the current pricing and budget might preclude support of the 2011 results.

For transfer pricing purposes, it is generally accepted that limited risk companies such as Bolid Manufacturing should realize a net profit. Unplanned losses may be supported, but it is unlikely that the Canada Revenue Agency would accept planned losses.

As Bolid is currently budgeting an operating loss of 7.3%, CRA might well argue that its prices are not arm's length. It could then adjust the transfer prices and perhaps impose penalties.

Sample 3

In order to complete the statement of adjustments which I received from the lawyer today there is a couple of questions that I need some information from you. Did you continue to rent out the property from Feb - Oct, 2009? If yes, I need the total rents collected for 2009 and if anyone withheld the non-resident tax, the name of the person who collected it and how much. For the 2009 rents could you send me a summary of the total rents collected plus all the expenses you have paid during the year. A summary similar to the one for the 2008 taxes would be fine. Thanks.

Comments

In the section on email, I talked about the fact that too often we treat business messages more casually when they are delivered by email. That's what seems to have happened with this sample, and the result is a confusing bundle of requests, lumped together with no consideration for grammar or logical flow. Not only might the recipient be confused, but the written message wouldn't do the firm's image any good!

Rewrite

I received the Statement of Adjustments from the lawyer today. In order to complete it, I need the following information from you:

1. Did you continue to rent out the property from

February to October 2009?

2. If so, please advise me of the total rent collected for 2009.

3. If non-resident tax was withheld, please advise me of the amount collected and the name of the person who collected it.

4. Please send me a summary of rents and expenses for 2009, similar to the one you provided for 2008.

As we should complete the Statement of Adjustment by the end of next week, I would appreciate receiving this information by Friday afternoon. Thanks.

Sample 4

We have reviewed the letter dated May 14, 2010 (the "Letter") sent to you by the Canada Revenue Agency (the "CRA") regarding amounts disallowed in your 2009 Individual Income Tax Return (the "Return") for failure to qualify as medical expenses and will not be used to determine your medical expense tax credit. You requested that we provide you with our comments regarding the CRA's position on this matter. Our advice is based on our understanding of the existing provisions of the Income Tax Act (Canada) (the "ITA"), the Income Tax Act Regulations (the "ITR") and the current administrative policies of the CRA as well as the facts and assumptions set out herein. Please advise us immediately if you are aware of any errors or omissions.

Comments

Whew! My brain is reeling already, and this is just the introduction!

There are two topics here: the summary of what was in the CRA's letter and the basis of the advice. Therefore, there should be two paragraphs.

The combination of high-flown language, overenthusiastic definition of terms and too many words results in a pompous tone and a boring message. This doesn't bode well for the rest of this five-page letter!

Rewrite

> *We have reviewed the May 14, 2010 letter to you from the Canada Revenue Agency ("CRA"). The letter states that certain amounts claimed in your 2009 tax return do not qualify as medical expenses and will, therefore, not be used to determine your medical expense tax credit. You have asked for our comments on the CRA's position.*
>
> *Our advice is based not only on the provisions of the Income Tax Act (Canada) (the "Act"), the Income Tax Act Regulations (the "Regulations") and current CRA administrative policies, but also on the facts and assumptions set out below. If you know of any errors or omissions in the latter, therefore, please let us know immediately.*

Sample 5

I have looked at the T4's prepared by your former bookkeeper for 2009 as well as the letter of June 15 you have received from the Canada Revenue Agency ("CRA"). The amount due arises out of the difference between the CPP deductions that were reported on your 2009 T4 ($615.76) and the actual correct amount stated by CRA. The CPP pensionable earnings were $51,769.23. Based on the pensionable earnings, CRA has calculated that the CPP should have been $1,943.17. This is correct based on the pensionable earnings reported. The difference is $1,327.41. CRA is now demanding that you remit the employee and employer (which must match the employee portion) portions of CPP, which results in a total amount payable by you of $2,654.82, plus interest and penalties of $1,221.06. The total amount now owing is, therefore, $3,917.42. The T4 prepared for you by CRA reflects this amount for CPP.

Comments

When you must set out a series of figures resulting from a calculation, the narrative paragraph is not usually the best choice. It's much clearer to set it out like the arithmetical calculation it is. I've also performed the usual fluff removal.

Rewrite

I have reviewed the June 15 letter from the Canada

Revenue Agency ("CRA"), as well as the T4s prepared by your former bookkeeper.

The CRA calculates (and we confirm) the amount owing as follows:

Pensionable earnings	*$51,769.23*
Correct CPP	*$ 1,943.17*
Reported CPP	*$ 615.76*
Difference	*$ 1,327.41*
Total employee and employer portions (must be equal)	*$ 2,654.82*
Interest and penalties	*$ 1,221.06*
Total amount payable	*$ 3,875.88*

The T4 prepared for you by CRA reflects the correct CPP amount.

This is just a small sampling of how even a short passage can be clarified and improved by editing.

If you master the art of self-editing, you can put your initial thoughts into words faster and more confidently because you know the post-edit version will take care of any shortcomings.

Simplifying the Complex

As I said in the beginning, many of the written messages you must convey are complex, and often they are directed at people who don't understand the principles behind them. After all, that's why you are explaining them.

Following are three examples of typical explanations by accountants to clients, followed by my comments and simplified versions. Again I remind you there is more than one way to write any message and these may not even be the best. But in each case the simplified version would serve the client much better than the original.

Mr. Johnson's Capital Cost Allowance

You have received a request for an opinion from a lawyer regarding her client's tax situation.

First version

Dear Ms McKenna:

You have asked us to give our opinion on the tax situation of your client Arthur Johnson with regard to the home located at 953 Palm Lane, of which he is the sole owner. Following is a summary of our findings.

Mr. Johnson purchased the Palm Lane house as a rental property four years ago for a total expenditure of $575,000, determined at that time to consist of $175,000 for land and $400,000 for the building. He immediately rented the units to tenants who are two brothers and their families, each occupying one of the apartments. Since the purchase of the property, he has maintained a net rental income of $4,000 per month from these two apartments ($2,000 from each apartment.)

The house is a Class 1 depreciable property under the CCA depreciable asset classes as defined by the Canada Revenue Agency (CRA). As such, it is entitled to a capital cost allowance (CCA) at the rate of 4% on a declining balance basis. In the first year, the CCA is computed at half the applicable rate, ie 2%.

When he purchased the house, Mr. Johnson installed a new furnace in the house, for a total expenditure of $15,000. As a capital asset, installed in the same Class 1 building, this amount is amortizable at 4% per year on a declining balance basis. Again, in the first year, the CCA is computed at half the applicable rate, ie 2%.

Last year, the personal circumstances of the tenants were such that they were forced to surrender their occupancy. Economic circumstances at that time rendered it impossible for Mr. Johnson to find replacement tenants for some time. In total, both apartments were vacant for a period of approximately six months. Mr. Johnson decided to make the most of the unfortunate circumstance of the empty apartments, and took the opportunity to undertake renovations in both apartments, with the hope of increasing their rental value in the long term. The total cost of the renovations in both apartments was $40,000.

As part of the Class 1 building, this capital expenditure is also entitled to a capital cost allowance (CCA) on a declining balance basis, subject to the limitation of one-half of the allowance in year one.

Taking into account the CCA on the original purchase of the property as well as the purchase of the furnace and the recent renovations, in the current year Mr. Johnson's total CCA allowances on the building, the *furnace and the renovation, therefore, amounts to $15,793. He is entitled to deduct this amount from his current year's income for tax purposes.*

Please do not hesitate to contact the undersigned should you have any questions or concerns with regard to your client's situation.

Sincerely,

The Simplification

To simplify this example, ask yourself the following questions:

1. What is the most important point you want to make?
2. How much background detail is necessary, given that the letter is to Mr. Johnson's lawyer?
3. What level of jargon is appropriate?
4. Is the information set out clearly and concisely?

My answers would be as follows:

1. She needs to know the total amount of CCA Mr. Johnson can claim.
2. As the information was provided by the reader in the first place, only a minimal amount of detail is necessary.
3. Although it's possible that the lawyer is familiar with tax jargon and terminology, you should still

keep it to a minimum. Why? Because he or she is quite likely to quote your letter chapter and verse when passing advice along to the client, who may not know the jargon at all.

4. It's not as obscure as some I've seen; however, it could be made more clear and more concise at the same time by taking out the fluff—lots and lots of fluff! Note the way I set out the figures as a table. Explaining figures in a narrative paragraph forces readers to work them out as they read, while setting them out as a table makes them immediately clear.

The Rewrite

Dear Ms McKenna:

As requested, here are our findings on the tax position of your client Arthur Johnson with regard to the house at 95 Palm Lane.

Mr. Johnson purchased the house as a rental property four years ago for $575,000 (land $175,000, building $400,000). Both units are rented, for a total rental income of $4,000 per month.

CRA defines this as a Class 1 building for purposes of capital cost allowance ("CCA"), making it eligible for CCA of 4% on a declining basis. In the first year, however, the CCA is calculated at half that rate, or 2%.

At the same time as he purchased the house, Mr.

Johnson installed a new furnace at a cost of $15,000.

Last year, both tenants moved out. Being unable to rent the apartments immediately, Mr. Johnson took advantage of the vacancy to carry out renovations at a total cost of $40,000.

As capital assets in a Class 1 building, both the furnace and the renovations are entitled to a CCA of 4% on a declining basis. Again, in the year of purchase, the CCA is computed at half the allowance rate, or 2%.

The amounts are set out in the table below.

Year	Cost	Adds	50% of Adds	CCA Base	CCA Rate	CCA	Closing Cost
1	—	415,000	207,500	207,500	4%	8,300	$406,700
2	$406,700	—	—	406,700	4%	16,268	$390,432
3	$390,432	—	—	390,432	4%	15,617	$374,815
4	$374,815	40,000	20,000	394,815	4%	15,793	$399,022

Please feel free to call me with any questions you may have about your client's tax situation.

Sincerely,

Ms Robinson's Stock Option

Your client Arabella Robinson has asked you for tax advice around her stock option. She wants to exercise the option now but not sell the shares until next year.

First version

Dear Ms Robinson:

You have asked me to advise you on the tax situation that would arise should you elect to exercise your stock option today but not sell the shares until next year. As I understand it, following are details of the option grant.

Your employer is Orion Widgets Inc., which is defined as a Canadian Controlled Private Corporation ("CCPC"). Orion Widgets Inc. granted you a stock option of 100,000 shares as part of your compensation package for the year 2008. The shares were at that time trading for $2 each, and this is your exercise price in respect of the options, making the total value of the shares $200,000 on the grant date.

Orion's shares are now trading at a price of $5 each. Thus, the value of the 100,000 shares is now $500,000. You can acquire the 100,000 shares for an exercise price of $200,000, and because the value of the shares acquired would be $500,000, then a $300,000 option benefit would arise.

However, you are not planning to sell the shares this year, but hold them until next year when you plan to sell them. Tax on the option benefit occurs in the year that the shares are sold. You should bear in mind that the price of the shares might well drop before you sell them, making your revenue from the sale lower. If this results in a loss on the sale of the shares, this will be classed as a capital loss. The benefit is considered income from employment. Capital losses can only be applied against capital gains, so in your case such a capital loss cannot be used to reduce the amount of your income for tax purposes. It can, however, be carried back three years or carried forward indefinitely, so you may be able to take advantage of it in a future year when you have a capital gain against which to apply it.

It is therefore our recommendation that you do not exercise your option until you are ready to sell the shares in order to avoid paying tax on a higher amount than you actually realize on the sale.

We trust this information is what you require. Should you have any questions or concerns, please do not hesitate to contact the undersigned.

Sincerely,

The Simplification

This message can be divided into three categories of information:

- The facts and figures of the stock option
- The amount of the taxable benefit and how it is calculated

- The advice to delay exercising the option until she is ready to sell the shares

It would certainly simplify the message if we made these divisions clear with sub-headings.

Finally, examine your words and cut out fluff and redundancy.

The Rewrite

Dear Ms Robinson:

As you requested, following is our opinion on the tax consequences of exercising your option today and selling the shares next year.

Option Details

Your employer, Orion Widgets Inc., is a Canadian Controlled Private Corporation ("CCPC"). In 2008 Orion granted you a stock option of 100,000 shares, which were then trading for $2 each. The total exercise price is therefore $200,000.

Orion's shares are now trading at $5 each, making the value of the 100,000 shares $500,000. Therefore, should you exercise the option today, you would realize a benefit of $300,000.

How the Tax Is Calculated

Stock options are granted on a specific day, usually at the market value of the shares on that day. The idea is to exercise the option at that price on a date when the shares are priced higher, thus realizing a gain, or benefit. This benefit, however, is taxable.

If you exercise the option on the shares of a CCPC, such as Orion, but do not sell the shares that year, you are allowed to defer the benefit until you do sell them.

Our Advice re Timing

You are considering exercising the option this year, but selling the shares next year when you will have a need for the cash. The problem is that if the share price drops in the meantime, you will realize less cash but will still have to pay tax calculated on the share value at the time of exercise. If you were to actually realize a loss on the sale of the shares, you would not be able to apply that capital loss against the opton benefit, as the latter is considered employment income and capital losses can only be applied against capital gains.

We therefore recommend that you do not exercise the option until you are ready to sell the shares.

If you have any questions, please give me a call

Sincerely,

Mr. Gonzalez Sells His Cottage

Your client, Manuel Gonzalez, purchased a summer cottage ten years ago for $85,000, including real estate fees and repairs. He has asked what tax liability will result from his intended sale of the cottage to his nephew.

First version

> *Dear Mr. Gonzalez,*
>
> *You have asked us for our opinion on your tax situation for the current year with regard to the sale of your cottage to your nephew, Jorge. It is our understanding that you purchased the cottage ten years ago for $85,000 and will be selling it to Jorge for $150,000. However, his financial position allows him to pay only $50,000 this year, with the balance of $100,000 next year.*
>
> *You will realize a total capital gain of $65,000 on this transaction (i.e. the selling price less the original purchase price, which was net of fees and some repair costs. This is called the Adjusted Cost Base.)*
>
> *Because you are receiving only $50,000 in the current tax year, you can take a reserve on the remaining $100,000 until next year. The amount of the reserve is calculated as the lesser of two formulas, as follows:*
>
> *1. (Proceeds still to be paid divided by total proceeds) x total capital gain*
> *OR*

2. 1/5 of total capital gain x (4 minus the number of preceding tax years ending after the sale)

Using your figures, therefore, the calculations are as follows:

1. ($100,000 divided by $150,000) x $65,000 = $43,333

2. 1/5 of $65,000 x (4-0) = $52,000

The lesser of the two is the first equation. Therefore, in the current tax year you may shelter $43,333 of your capital gain and report only $21,667 as income.

Following the same formulas for next year:

1. ($0 divided by $150,000) x $65,000 = $0

2. 1/5 of $65,000 x (4-1) = $39,000

Once again the lesser is the first equation, which is zero. Therefore you cannot take any reserve next year, and you will have to report the entire remaining $43,333.

Should you have any questions with regard to the above, please do not hesitate to contact the undersigned at your convenience.

Yours sincerely,

The Simplification

This is a case of cutting out fluff and using simpler language a lay person could understand.

The Rewrite

Dear Mr. Gonzalez:

The following sets out your tax situation on the sale of your cottage to your nephew, Jorge Gonzalez.

The capital gain

1. You purchased the cottage ten years ago for a net total of $85,000.

2. This month you are selling it to your nephew Jorge for $150,000, resulting in a capital gain of $65,000.

Tax calculation

Jorge will pay $50,000 immediately and the remaining $100,000 next year. As you are receiving only part of the proceeds this year, you can report part of your capital gain this year, deferring the rest until next year when you receive the balance of the proceeds.

The amount of the reserve is calculated as the lesser of:

1. (Proceeds still to be paid/total proceeds) x total capital gain

OR
2. 1/5 of total capital gain x (4 minus the number of preceding tax years ending after the sale)

Your calculation for this year is as follows:

1. ($100,000 divided by $150,000) x $65,000 = $43,333

OR
2. 1/5 of $65,000 x (4-0) = $52,000

Since the lesser of the two is the first, you may defer $43,333 of your capital gain and report only $21,667 as income this year.

After you receive the balance of the proceeds next year, the calculation will be:

1. ($0/$150,000) x $65,000 = $0
2. 1/5 of $65,000 x (4-1) = $39,000

Once again the lesser result is the first, which is zero. Therefore you cannot take any further reserve, and you must report the remainder of your capital gain, i.e. $43,333, as income for next year.

If you require any further information, please give me a call and I will be glad to help.

Sincerely,

In Closing

As I said in the introduction, this book is not intended to be a comprehensive study of business writing for accountants. My intent was to create a book from which you could learn enough universal principles of business writing, couched in terms taken directly from your world, that you can apply in all writing situations you come across in your job. In fact, a *Short Painless Guide*.

I suggest you don't try to do everything at once. Instead, take the principles I've discussed one at a time and apply it to your writing process. As you incorporate them, you should see a definite improvement in your writing, in the impact of your written messages and in your use of the written word as an effective professional tool.

As you become more adept at using the information I've provided, you'll also find you write more easily and quickly. This, in turn, will increase your productivity.

I believe that by improving your writing skills, you will become a better accountant. If this book helps you do that, it will have met its objective.

I welcome your comments and feedback on the book, as well as any suggested additions to future editions. My email address is hwilkie@mhwcom.com. Please write in!

About the Author

Helen Wilkie is a professional speaker, workshop leader and writer based in Toronto, Canada. She specializes in communication at work, including why it is important as well as the individual skills, such as business writing.

Helen has conducted writing courses, workshops and webinars for some of the top accounting firms and professional accounting bodies in Canada. In the course of this work, she has become familiar with the particular writing challenges of the profession as well as its jargon and terminology—although she is the first to admit she can sometimes still be baffled!

Based on comments from her clients, she felt there was a need for a book on business writing specifically for accountants. Being familiar also with their lack of time, she decided it should be short, and this book is the result.

The following pages contain information on some of Helen's professional development programs.

Business Writing Programs

Effective Business Writing for Accountants

A six-part, hands-on course for groups of up to 25 accountants, with content tailored specifically to the needs of the profession and even of specific firms when requested.

This course is usually delivered in six weekly sessions, each lasting two hours. However, for clients who find this impractical, usually for geographical reasons, the content can be adapted for delivery in 1-1/2 days.

Helen's 9 Rules for Better Business Writing

A 60-90 minute session developed for delivery at conferences, also appropriate for the popular "lunch and learn" format.

While the content is largely generic, many of the examples used to illustrate points are drawn from the accounting world. This program, while not a substitute for the full hands-on course, can serve as a useful introduction to stimulate interest among your professionals.

Simplifying the Complex

Can be delivered as a 60-minute lunch and learn or conference workshop, or expanded to half a day with hands-on exercises.

This program is designed specifically for accountants.

Business Writing Course on CD

A self-study course whose content is generic, but easily adaptable to the specific needs of users.

As the name suggests, it comes on a CD, and the material is delivered through a combination of live-action video and PowerPoint slides. This program may be used as a standalone course for individuals or as an adjunct to the main course, allowing participants to use it as an ongoing learning tool.

Coaching

One-on-one writing coaching for accountants at all levels.

This can be delivered in person or in a combination of telephone and e-mail contact.

For more information on Helen's writing and other communication programs, visit:

www.mhwcom.com

www.masteringbusinesswriting.com

www.Communi-keys.com

To book Helen for your conference or other professional development needs, call 416-966-5023 or email hwilkie@mhwcom.com